# PLEIADIAN SPIRALS OF LIGHT

## CLIMB THE LADDER AND MANIFEST YOUR DREAMS

Climb the ladder of the energy centers and accomplish all of your dreams. Opening your energy centers is what the Hindu calls chakras can transmute your cell metabolism dramatically changing your energetic tissues of your body. To gain success and true power, we must climb the ladder within our energy body. With this workbook, you can gain better spiritual awareness and better health and approve all aspects of your life.

# ABOUT THE AUTHOR

Ed Russo has taken an interest in metaphysics after a UFO encounter in the early years of his life. He has over 10 years of studying the esoteric sciences and nature religions. He has been a member of many spiritual and esoteric groups. He studies the teachings from the Kabbalah Centre. In addition to being a ULC Minister, he has also lectured on metaphysics and human development, written articles for a mental health news brochure. He was a guest on Blogtalk radio hosted by Royce Holleman on the paranormal.

# TO WRITE TO THE AUTHOR

If you wish to contact the author or would like more information about this book, please write to the author in care of Illuminated Publications, and we will forward the request. Both the author and publisher would like to hear from readers, learning from your enjoyment and benefit from the book. To write to the author, write to:

Ed Russo
c/o ILLUMINATED PUBLICATIONS
goldenilluminati@yahoo.com


For information on other books can be found on the website.
http://www.lulu.com/spotlight/dark_corvus

# PLEIADIAN SPIRALS OF LIGHT

## Workbook

**Ed Russo**

ILLUMINATED PUBLICATIONS, PITTSBURGH

Also by Ed Russo

THE ILLUMINATI CODE: Mystery of the New World Order

THE ILLUMINATI CODE 2: The Apocalypse Rises
THE MERMIAD'S CURSE
DEAD AND GONE
THE SCIENCE OF BUSINESS: The secret to a successful
Business
THE PLEIADIAN PAPERS
MUSHROOM MADNESS
Published by
ILLUMINATED PUBLICATIONS
Copyright © 2013
ISBN 978-1-304-28573-7

Dedicated to all who wants to grow

# Table of contents

# INTRODUCTION

There are Masters of Light who have the ability to create all their dreams. Some are from this planet, some are from other worlds. Who are these Masters of Light? They are those who overcame the limitations that hold the rest of humanity back. These Emissaries of Light are one with the God-Self. The human body has major physical organs that we are all aware of. Those are the heart, lungs, liver and other major organs that is necessary to live. We also have an astral body or what some call a soul body. The astral body also has major organs to, very much like major physical organs in the human body. These organs in the astral body are spirals of energy centers that the Hindu Yogi calls Chakras. The Egyptians call them the Seven Powers. The Chinese call it the Thrusting Vessel. The Chinese focus more on the energy line than the energy centers. These spirals are like funnels. The front and back of the centers that are vortexes are considered to be one. The funnels are coming out of both sides and meeting in the middle. This is considered the heart of the Centers. The front side represents the person's feelings and the backside represents their will. When these centers are weak it affects the person's mental and physical health. It is also the cause of all our successes and failures in life is based upon the health of our energy centers. This workbook will show you what to do to strengthen your energy centers to change your life. This is the first step into becoming a Master of Light.

The idea is to recognize the God Self. The Pleiadian and other Emissaries of Light are in contact with the God Self. They are Masters of Light and are here to let mankind here to realize that they also can become Masters of Light. Before one can become a Master of Light, you first have to understand what Light is. This work book is designed to help you change and raise your vibrations. To have happiness in life, one vibration must be aligned to reflect that. One must take full personal responsibility for ones actions. That includes your thoughts and vibrations.

Desire is the force that drives everything. Desire is Love, and it is from love that all originates from. Love is Light, and there is nothing else in existence but Light. Two systems have been squabbling at each other. Those two systems are religion and science.. The extraterrestrials contact that has been taking place over time is designed to create a bridge between science and religion. The Source which is Light is what many religions call God. Gravity is Desire. The Law of Love and the Law of Gravity are the same. It is the force that causes likes to attract likes. Similar things bond to similar things. When a planet is in space it is weightless. Whenever matter is in the place of its birth, it belongs there, and therefore, in balance. It floats in its balanced field. In that position it is weightless in respect to anything else in the universe. When another body comes near it matter is out of balanced as it creates a bond causing the measurement in weight. The more the mass is similar to the other mass, the stronger the bond and the more it weighs. Gravity doesn't just pull in one direction. It pulls in either direction. Water vapor goes up and collects and become clouds. That is gravity pulling water vapor upwards towards its similarity which is the gases that make up the atmosphere.

Gravity causes motion and motion creates electricity. Electricity is the force to create material manifestation. Material manifestations are electrical disturbances in a vacuum. Electricity causes those disturbances. Electricity manifest in polarity as female and male as electricity spirals around a black hole. The electrical current for example must have a positive and negative flow of ions. Without one polarity, there can be no electricity. The male (positive polarity) and female (negative polarity) must be present for anything to manifest. In space gravity which is desire creates electricity in a vacuum. This vacuum is disturbed and hydrogen is the matter that is created. The hydrogen spirals together. As it spirals together it is called a Nebula. As the Nebula continues to spiral together the friction causes heat and eventually a star is born. As this sphere continues to manifest and hold together due to cold space that compresses it and heat that expands it, the frequency next in line that is produced is the element helium. Each octave on the energy keyboard owes its existence to the combination of positive and negative vibrations. Each keyboard of energy is a combination of positive and negative vibrations. Therefore there are reactions that occur between these vibrations. That means each vibrational field is a product created by a union of two vibrations. Each vibration of energy of the keyboard is an extension of the one preceding it. All vibrations from the highest (cosmic rays) to the lowest (physical matter) on the vibratory plane, have frequencies that are multiples of those corresponding to each note on the musical scale. There exists a single scale that is composed of seven major divisions that repeats itself from the infinitely smaller unit to the infinitely larger universe. Like the music scale has C, D, E, F, G, A and B in where each octave composes the different scales, well it's the same on the energy keyboard.

Musicians noted that there are 9 auditory scales in music that correspond to the musical keyboard. The energy keyboard has 144 totals of octaves. That means on the scale from its most sublime manifestation, it is repeated 144 times, therefore giving a total of 1008 major notes for the energy keyboard.

The Law of the Triangle

The Law of the Triangle is that nothing can manifest without the negative and positive polarity. The two polarities manifest the third point which forms the triangle. There are three planes of existence. All creation takes form according to the Law of the Triangle; the number 3. The three planes are concrete by the number 9. For 9 is the only number to interface and penetrate into one of the three planes. On the three planes exist the material, mental and astral. All the other numbers such as 1-8 are subjected to their temporal spatial plane of manifestation. 9 allow direct passage to the planes while 1-8 requires special preparation which is more complex.

When it comes to the cycle of nine the initial vibration has a frequency with a theosophical reduction of 0 or 9. Even though the number 9 is considered uneven, the corresponding vibration is not negative, but neutral. The number 9 is a neutral number because it marks the end of a cycle and beginning of another in the creation of a vibration condition. The number 9 is associated with 0 in mathematical derivations. These numbers do not change the total that is obtained in theses calculations. Such as this example: $5+9 = 14 = 1+4 = 5+0$ , which shows 0 plays the same role as 9 in numerical function. Even in multiplication it applies. Any reduction of the product of multiplication by 9 always results in 9. Example: $4 \times 9 = 36 = 3+6 = 9$.

Vibrations do not have periods corresponding to all numbers from 1 to infinity, but instead have periods that correspond to the interval between 0 and 9. Therefore all the octaves of energy from cosmic rays to physical matter consist of the combination of positive and negative frequencies based on the cyclic periodicity expressed by the number 9. That's why the number system is 0-9 and then repeats itself as 10 which the theosophical reduction is 1, and the next number 11 theosophical reduction is 2 and so on. This repeat goes on for eternity. The theosophical reduction will always be the same. In multiplication its 0 thru 9

$10,11,12,13,14,15,16,17,18,19 = 1,2,3,4,5,6,7,8,9,1$ theosophical reduction

$10,11,12,13,14,15,16,17,18,19 - 0,1,2,3,4,5,6,7,8,9$ tr by multiplication

Since there are three planes of existence, the triangle is used to symbolize that. Space symbolizes the circle. Space is curved and the circle is 360 degrees which the theosophical reduction equals 9. The circle is infinite and finite. The circle is the completion of nine and zero. It is the Ouroboros, the dragon or serpent eating its tail.

Image from www.aeriagames.com

Since the triangle symbolizes the three, which is the father (positive), mother (negative) polarity and child, the triangle is used inside the circle. Since all is polarized, the triangle then polarizes itself as two interlaced triangles. The interlaced triangles are a hexagram. Each point of the hexagram within the circle manifest circles around each point. Each of these circles are boundaries create. Within each of these boundaries is the triangle which is a point of each hexagram. Since everything polarizes, those triangles become interlaced. This creation of boundaries will continue on infinity making smaller circles. Therefore you have Infinity within the finite, creating a endless amounts of replicate objects within the original circle.

Therefore each circle appears to be an isolated structure with its own information. But exactly each individual circle has all the exact information as the whole. Now this large circle that appears to be isolated from space outside it, if you zoomed out you will see that it is a circle inside another circle. You would see it gets larger and larger infinitely. It would be like two mirrors facing each other where the reflections go infinitely in both directions.

Each individual circle has the information of all, what determines its individuality is code within the script. That is the number of protons that is inside the atom. These numbers determine the frequency of each circle.

When an atom has one proton then the element is hydrogen, as this continues the next set of atoms have two protons, that element is then helium. This continues on. Each set of atoms that manifest has one extra proton inside than the one previous. Each proton has all the information as the universe itself does. The proton itself is a universe on a sub-atomic scale. It is a fractal of the whole. We live in a holographic universe. Like a hologram, light shines through a zone plate that has the original recording of an image. The light that shines through creates a three dimensional hologram. The hologram may have multiple images that appear separate. The truth is that it comes from light shining through the zone plate. The world we live in is just one light that creates holograms that appear separate. The reason why we don't go through holograms around us like the hologram shining from a zone plate is because we are holograms too. The material world we experience, the holograms project an electromagnetic field. When the electromagnetic field in both objects repels each other it appears solid. Our hand cannot pass through it. When the electromagnetic field does not repel each other then our hand passes through it like the holograms projected from a zone plate. When our electromagnetic field comes in contact with another electromagnetic field that isn't in phase, it sends electrical impulses to the brain giving us the feeling of the sense of touch. Our minds create what we expect even if it isn't so. The universe is somewhat plastic where it can be altered. We have holograms in our brain much like images on a TV. We see what we expect.. Tai Chi Masters have a exercise that shows how limitations are create in the mind. They realize this and learn to overcome limitations to the point where they can knock a crowd down with the wave of their hand. Here is an exercise to show that solidity and obstacles are an illusion. Clasp left hand over wrist of right hand. Press up with right arm with all your strength as you equally press down with your left. Now feel tension in both. Now keep tension between both, but focus all awareness of tension in right arm without releasing. Now that you feel the tension in shoulder and arm, move the left arm away. Notice that when you first moved the left hand away the right hand didn't move? That is because you still thought you was pushing the right arm up against the left that was no longer there.

As long as you think the obstacle is there you freeze up and cannot do anything else. This is example with the arm. In life generally obstacles are what are created in our mind. Therefore the things that hold us back only exist in the mind.

Everything spirals. As I said before, electricity spirals as it moves around the center of the blackhole. The negative ions and positive ions move in two directions. One moves inward while the other moves outward. As you see the Galaxy spirals around the blackhole, the reason why you see black space between each spiral bands is because the blackness is spiraling in the opposite direction than the spiral of bands that are visible. The energy that spirals inward is invisible to the human eye. The mother (negative) light radiate by reaching out from the center of the blackhole to give birth to countless of stars and planets by unfolding them from the centering seed. The arms of gravitating father (positive) light pull spirally inward from the stars toward the poles of the center of the blackhole. Gravitation is the male polarity of Creation. Gravity folds toward the seed. Radiation is the female polarity of Creation. Radiation unfolds from the seed. This balance of interchange between father-mother waves of gravitation and radiation is basis for all created things. It is the principle of the two way equal giving which manifest the quality of Love in the Light of the Singularity.

This spiraling takes place in everything. The first element which is hydrogen spirals together as the Nebula. The suns are formed due to the spiraling of gases. The atom itself is spiraling. The momentum of the spiraling is what keeps the suns and planets to continue to rotate.

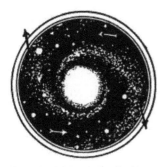

Russell's Curve Electric Universe

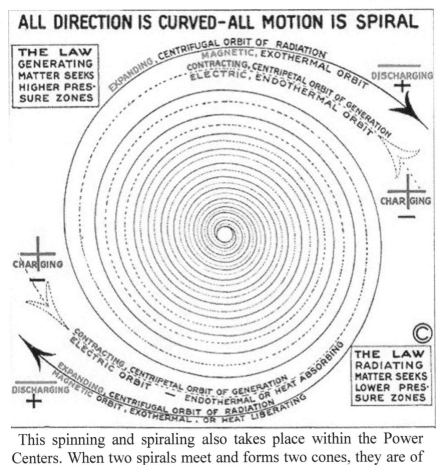

This spinning and spiraling also takes place within the Power Centers. When two spirals meet and forms two cones, they are of two different polarities that become mates. The spirals rotate to the still centering shafts where the cones meet. In the Power Centers in the astral body the two spiraling cone mates meet at the centering shaft. One spiral cone (mother) is associated with feelings. The other cone (father) is associated with will. It is the will that impregnates the feelings and the feelings give birth to manifestation. Here is example of mating cones in figure 7.

ANTI-CLOCKWISE

CLOCKWISE

Fig 7

Directions of spiral
motion never reverses

The two spiraling cones together is a vortex. The spiraling cone in the front of the body of the Power Center is the feelings (mother) and the cone in the back of the body associated with will (father). The will must be exercised so that the will impregnates the feelings. It is the feelings that give birth to manifestation.

# THE FIRST SPIRAL
## (Element *Earth*)

We all know that the Physical body has major organs, such as the heart, liver, spleen, lungs as an example. Within our astral body we also have major organs. These are the Power Centers. First Spiral is the first Power Center. It is located near the anus at the base of the spine. It is associated with the element Earth. This Power Center is about survival. Here is a correspondent of the symbolism of this power center.

**Element:** Earth
**Function:** survival
**Glands:** adrenals
**Unbalances:** Obesity, constipation, hemorrhoids, money issues
**Color:** red
**Sephira:** Malkuth

This first spiral is associated with survival. When our Power Centers within our soul is plugged into the physical body our Power Centers are strong. We are more grounded. When strong, you love your career, and you no longer judge yourself, because you always feel loved and wanted by your friends. You have more than enough. You feel blessed and have much gratitude.

When this Power Center is weak, one feels trapped in an unwanted career. They feel that they don't have enough money. The thought of giving away money whether it is to pay bills or as a gift brings feelings of dread.

One becomes a tight-ass and anal-retentive. The one who is a tight-ass doesn't like to spend money or give any away. The unbalance of this Power Center also brings constipation, and Freud considered anal-retentive as a child who refuses to move his bowels. The use of this phrase is used to describe someone who will not let go of his ego driven impulse to dominate others.

This person's self-esteem is low that they have to inflate their ego to compete with others to feel worthy. They are always in a state of self-judgment and always feel that they have to live up to some standard. Those who suffer from over weight judge themselves by constant questioning of one self. When this Power Center is weak one has tendency to seek outside approval for one's self worth.

When we don't feel worthy, we are not grounded. The reason is because when one doesn't feel worthy they question themselves. One questions if they are stable enough to stand on their own two feet. One then has unrealistic thinking while not grounded in the world that is around them. One asks do they have the right to be here to, to take up space. This thinking leads to one thinking that they don't deserve to have what they need to survive.

When one doesn't think they deserve to have what they need to survive, the feelings involve makes it harder to survive. That vibration creates situations that lead to financial hardship and other things needed for survival. Many drug addicts and alcoholics struggle with this mind set. They feel that they are not worthy to have their needs therefore escape through drug use. They are not grounded and don't believe they are stable enough to stand on their own two feet, so they rely on drugs or alcohol for support. While using drugs or abusing alcohol one holds on to erroneous beliefs that they will be worthy after they quit, instead of realizing that one is already worthy just because they are alive. This individual struggles with their self worth, then when they may become clean and sober, many relapse because they still don't feel worthy of having their needs met because life still seems overwhelming.

When it comes to survival the adrenal glands plays a part. When we feel like we are in danger the adrenal glands secrete adrenaline which triggers the fight or flight response. In this survival mode we react quickly only focusing on this situation. In the modern world the fight or flight response is mostly unnecessary. We are not in the world where we have to constantly be on the look out for wild animals or a warring enemy tribe out to get us. Many of the fears we have today are irrational. Those irrational fears may

2

be anxiety over losing our jobs, fear of loss of love relationship etc. The flight or fight response cause one to either react in a aggressive or a submissive manner. Handling the situation in an assertive manner is how one solves the dilemma. Assertiveness would be taking the right actions that are needed to save your job or relationships. Assertiveness is how you get your needs met. Aggressiveness or passiveness never get needs met. When one is in the aggressive (fight) state, they may express their needs, but the aggressiveness puts others on the defense. This does nothing but backfire. Using force, whether it is by words or physical actions fail to achieve goals. Nature does not force. Love does not operate on force, aggression is force. For one to overcome these fears, one must acknowledge the God Within. When you know and recognize the God Within, then you know that you are worthy and deserve to have all the things necessary to live. Truly knowing this eliminates fear. Knowing this you know that everything that you need is at arms reach.

When this Power Center is strong we can live life without the need to measure up to some standard. We realize that we are not what we do, or have done.

There are exercises to help build resistance to the stress that cause the fight or flight response. One way is to increase your physical resistance to stress. Our convictions are held in the physical body. What ever our beliefs are is associated with body tension. Different beliefs tense certain areas of the physical body. It takes our body to tense in certain areas in order to hold on to our strong beliefs. Relaxing those tensions will help let go of those beliefs that may be creating fear. Some people are more vulnerable to stress than others due to this tension associated by their beliefs.

Examined and ask your self do you get stressed easier or less than others that you know. Mark down below which category that you fall into.

I seem calmer than most people _____

About the same as most people  _____

I seem to get more upset than most people I know _____

    If you marked the third, then there are techniques that you may want to help you deal with this better.

**Exercise:** People who do regular exercise tend to have less stress and anxiety than those who do not, research indicates. It doesn't matter if the exercise is aerobic or anaerobic. Whatever you pick do it regular. Regular exercise helps raise serotonin levels in the blood. This chemical gives sense of well being. Exercise also helps relieve tensions associated with beliefs that make you more stressed. Pick any exercise routine that you enjoy or can do. Remember to stretch and warm up first. Within the first four weeks you will notice the benefits. Exercise also elevates a healthy amount of testosterone which makes you more assertive. So don't worry ladies, you will still be feminine. Being assertive you will calmly take the actions that are needed to get things done. Passiveness or aggression doesn't. When one doesn't get needs met, it causes anger. Anger manifest in the form of hostility or depression. Depression is anger turned inward, instead of outward in a hostile aggressive manner. When we are calm, we can think clearer and find better answers to solve problems. Being overwhelmed hinders one from being able to see how to solve a situation.

**Healthy Eating:** when we eat food that isn't healthy while on the run, it doesn't help stress at all. Eating balance nutritional meals is what helps. Make simple choices such as eating a salad over some greasy French fries. Taking time to sit down and chew your food helps. It takes 20 minutes before the body to recognize it isn't hungry. That means no matter how much you eat, if it is eating before those 20 minutes is up, you will still feel hungry. Eat your vegetables and get protein. Protein can be from beans and nuts and lean meats. Try to cut down on sugar. Sugar has been known to cause a roller-coaster change in moods. Also watch your caffeine intake.. not only is caffeine addictive, it also stimulates the stress response. If you have anxiety or anger problems or trouble sleeping, one should then cut down on the use of caffeine products.

**Get enough sleep:** Getting enough sleep is essential. Many people don't get enough sleep and sleep deprivation contributes to higher levels of stress. Make sure that you have getting enough sleep at night is a major priority in your life. Most need about 8 hours asleep each night for top performance. Every individual is different. For best results have a regular bedtime and time that you wake up. Make sure that your sleeping environment is fit in terms of temperature, darkness and quiet. If you have trouble sleeping, you may want to consult your doctor.

**Live a balanced life:** Is your life balanced? Do you try to do too much during the day? If you are multi-tasking trying to do too many things at once, well then slow down. Trying to do too many things at once causes stress. Things can be overwhelming and you will feel yourself being pulled into aggressive, passive and or passive-aggressive behavior. Therefore slow down and realize there is no need to hurry. Taking actions to extend your life, then that relieves the stress of trying to get everything done at the moment. No one at the end of their life thinks, "darn, I wish I spent more time at work," slow down and plan ahead, and stop trying to do too many things at once.

# Examine your situations

Another way of reducing anxiety is to examine your situation. Sometimes we think our situations are far more threatening than they are.

Think of a situation that happens within the past few weeks that was small, but caused a big reaction for you. Write down the situation.

_____

_____

_____

We usually do not react to what's going on, but react to what we think is going on. If you overreacted to a small event or even what the event meant to you, write it down. Perhaps a friend didn't respond to you on facebook but you decided it meant she doesn't want to be bothered by you. Your emotional response isn't to her lack of response but to her not wanting to be your friend.

Judgments about what situations mean happen automatically usually without us being aware. We get upset and don't know why. The idea is to ask yourself what did the situation mean. Evaluate the meaning, substitute a different meaning if we think that we may be thinking unrealistically

Think about the stressful situation that you wrote down. What did the situation mean to you? What did it say about you, or the other person or the world that you live in?

_____

_____

_____

Are you a 100% sure that what you believe the situation meant to you is true? Is it possible that there may have been other reasons why the situation happens? List them.

_____

_____

_____

Are the alternative reasons less threatening than you thought? Most likely the answer is yes. When we are stressed, we tend to make matters worse. Our imaginations get carried away and we are consumed in unnecessary anxiety. We need to ask questions about why we are so anxious over situations. Check the one that applies to you.

__ **Is my life in danger?** The fight and flight response that is triggered from stress is designed to save our lives. Today we are most likely not in danger of our lives. Therefore ask "Is your life in danger from the situation that you make is so worked up about?" Most situations that we have so much anxiety over are not a life or death situation at all. When you realize that your life isn't in any danger, it can help you to let go of what has you so worked up.

__ **What is the worst thing that could happen?** We tend to get tensed up about things that are minor. We imagine the worst scenario. If what you feared did come true, can you live with yourself? If you can live with it, then you do not NEED the situation to work out the way you want it. It is just that you prefer that it would, but you don't NEED it. It's not the end of the world for example if such and such never speak to you again.

__ **Will tension help the situation?** Many times we are tense and feel that we need to be tense about the situation. Tension is only good for two things, which are to fight or to flee. Tension as I said earlier is caused by our convictions, those emotional beliefs that we feel that we need to hold onto. If we do not need to fight or run, then there is no need for tension. We can then let go of the tensions as it helps us let go of our beliefs.

**Three column list.** To explore other ways of thinking, you can use a three column list. In the first column, write down the incident. In the second column write down those automatic thoughts that you interpret that the incident is about. In the third column write what it may be about. Write a list of all possibilities.

Doing this exercise you may realize that you was just assuming things that wasn't so. You may realize that you were just overly thinking negative about something. This may help relieve anxiety about the situation when you realize that you are not threatened and it's more minor than you thought.

| Incident | Automatic Thoughts | Likely reasons |
|---|---|---|
| Josephine seems to be a little distance lately. | That means that she is about to leave me and then our relationship will end. | Maybe I'm just imagining that she is distance. |
| | That means that she must be tired of me and there is someone else. | Perhaps she is going through something and it has nothing to do with me. |
| | Maybe she just doesn't like me anymore and I turned out to be nothing but a great disappointment. | Perhaps maybe I shouldn't wear out my welcome and just ease up just a little. |
| | | Of course she still likes me, why wouldn't she, I'm fun to be around. I make her feel safe. |

Stress makes us more impulsive, it causes us to respond either too passively or too aggressively or in a passive aggressive way. Being calm then you can assertively pursue and take the action that is needed. This requires willpower.

Our automatic thoughts come from our childhood programming. This is why they are automatic. Many of them are unhealthy. The first Power Center spiral stores all of our survival information like a computer floppy disk. Automatic thoughts are like a computer responding to the information on a floppy disk. We all have part of the brain called the reptile brain. It survives on pleasure. You cannot fight it, like the force of gravity all you can do is accept the pull and work with it. The reptilian brain will do anything to survive even if it destroys the host. That host is your body. This is also called the chthonic mind. The reptilian brain can get its pleasure from food, fluids, oxygen, sex and nurturing. When it isn't being fed pleasures by these necessities, it will compensate for something else just to survive. This is when we become a slave by given into things that harm our well being. Working with the chthonic mind is to reprogram it so that it can get its pleasure from the necessities. Proper diet is how it gets pleasure from food, drinking enough fluids is how it gets pleasure from fluids. Exercising and proper breathing is how it gets its pleasure from oxygen. Having an orgasm once a week is healthy, even if it's self pleasure. This is how the reptilian brain gets its pleasure. Having a social life by connecting with others is how it gets its nurturing. It is about balance. Sometimes it isn't easy to feed the reptilian brain with these necessities due to our self sabotaging behavior because of how we feel about our right to be here. There is another way to reprogram the chthonic mind to change this. Auto suggestions is away to change our automatic thoughts. Chthonic means rooted within or under the earth. In Greek mythology it is the underworld. The chthonic mind is the deep unconscious aspect of our mind that drives all the choices we make when it comes to survival. In Greek mythology for example the underworld is where spirits of nature that is creativity animating men or manifest as a spirit of evil as a drive to destroy. Therefore the monsters inside us that lies in the deep, cannot be destroyed, they can only be tamed.

Autosuggestion is the art of manifesting things in your life by putting focus on them and repeating verbally or mentally what you want.

# I am

When it comes to auto-suggestions, words are very important. The wording and everything is important for success. The word "I AM" is a very powerful word. The word is the power of manifestation. For example if you want to become successful, to say, I am becoming successful wouldn't be appropriate. To say that affirmation is to program the mind of always becoming but never reaching success. Therefore the appropriate suggestion would be, "I am successful" current situations in one's life may debunk that suggestion saying in jest, "yeah right, successful, I don't think so." Get pass the debunking and by continuing repeatedly the suggestion, "I am Successful" then in time you will come to believe it. One must feel it and once you do, you will manifest in your life success. Another thing about the mind is that the mind does not negate. Words like no or not does not register in the mind. That is part of the reason when you tell someone not to do something, they do it anyway. For example if you are trying to lose weight, saying "I am not fat", is not appropriate. The mind picks up everything in that sentence except not. All the mind hears in that suggestion is 'I am fat" therefore one again must put what you want after the word I am, such as "I am thin". No matter how unrealistic this may appear this is how the mind works. The belief takes place in the mind first before it manifest in material reality. Whatever you want, you must feel that you already have it. Feel and believe that you have the money that you need. Realize that you deserve it. In time you will program the mind to accept it while your habits change to move towards what you believe that you deserve and desire. Your subconscious mind will give you the insight of what actions are needed to get the money that is coming. You may receive insight from sudden inspiration, it is important to act on the information that is coming to you. This flash of insight may be coming to you from the Cosmic. The Cosmic Intelligence is the link to the subconscious mind. This is also what one needs to do in anything else you want. If you want to lose weight see and feel that you are there.

Go somewhere quiet and say out loud the amount of money that you want. See the time limit and how you will serve in order to receive it. Write the amount down here.

_____

_____

_____

For example you want to accumulate $9000 by August 3rd. you agree to give service through sales on an online mail-order business. Repeat what you want and feel it every night and morning. This is how you reprogram scarcity to abundance. Too many of us feel we don't deserve or feel guilty if we take a day off of work, or feel guilty if someone even helps us with money.

## Our Body

When it comes to our body, we must be comfortable with our body before we can be comfortable with our inner self. One must be comfortable in their own skin. To master the first energy center is to heal our body. We must learn to accept, feel and love our body. This is a challenge, because many of us don't like what we see in the mirror. As we examine our body we see deeper parts of ourselves. Our body is the machine that receives all the information programmed into us. This programming comes from our genetics, food we eat, and our daily habits. All this reflects in the appearance of this body machine that we operate it. We must be in our body to love it. When it comes to losing weight one must first accept their body. If you are teething with hating how you look, you produce hormones that just cause you to gain more weight. Despising how you look just makes it much harder to change the weight issue. As I said before being grounded helps us be in our body. When it comes to diet, make sure you have enough protein. As I mention earlier exercise can help you be grounded. Meditation also helps you be in your body. The meditation that allows you to be in your body is to be aware of your body sensations.

Sit with back straight and unsupported. Roll your shoulders back with your chest out some. Make sure that you are not slumped over. Make sure your head is straight ahead like its being supported by a string on the ceiling. Relax. Inhale three deep breaths and relax. Sit and feel your body sensations. How do you feel inside? Feel where you may have tensions. Be aware of what you may be feeling. The tension may be triggering a fight or flight response. Be aware and feel it. Don't try to change it, just acknowledge and feel it.

# Money

Before we can move on to other Power Centers we have to first be grounded in the first Center. You cannot build a house on quicksand. You must have a solid foundation. There are many mystic addicts who ignore the material plane and compulsively buy all kinds of esoteric material to try to evolve, but meanwhile they cannot even pay their rent. If you are not comfortable with a roof over your head and don't know how you are going to pay rent or eat, you cannot reach Illumination. Part of growth is interacting with the world where you have the capacity to help yourself and others. We are not here to just sit on a mountain top and meditate without doing anything else. To do that is just escaping from reality just like one who uses drugs to escape.

When you are comfortable surviving to where you can really live, then you have more energy to pursue higher teachings, teachings that are in the realm of the psychic.

When you have money it builds self-confidence, which is necessary for self mastery. Having money also increases social power as it can cause others to submit humbly to you. It also allows you to take advantage of medical advances to better your health.

Here is some ways to help you build your relationship with mastering money. The idea is to have money work for you, instead of working for money.

**Make sure your income is more than your living expenses:** This is important first part. This gives you enough to work with. Before you can do anything you first have to have a source of income and enough left after you pay your monthly bills. First get a income, either through a career or business. Keep track of your income and expenses. List what you spend on groceries, car payments etcetera. For a career you can see what careers are worth it or not. There is the Occupational Outlook Handbook to look at. http:www.bls.gov/oco/home.htm

If you wish to start a business I have a book called *How to Get Your Business Pregnant* which is also renamed *The Science of Business: The secret to a Successful Business* that gives insight on starting a business.

**Reduce bad debt:** There is a difference between bad debt and good debt. Good debt is when you borrow money to make an investment that will profit, like a business or paying mortgage. Bad debt on the other hand is like the money you owe on credit cards. The idea here is to reduce bad debt. Bad debt prevents one from financial success and can cause a psychological handicap. Getting rid of bad debt will effect your emotions. You will start to have a sense of control, knowing that you can solve the problem.

List all your bad debt sources. How much you pay for food, if you have a credit card, write down how much you spend and interest rates.

After listing the bad debt, separate each debt and divide that amount by the minimum monthly payment you have to make. That will tell you how long it will take to pay off the debt, minus the interest.

The debt that is the smallest amount of time to pay, make that your first choice to pay off.

Now pay the minimum that you have to on everything but your number one thing you chose. Total the entire minimum for everything and take 10% of that and add it to your monthly payment to your top choice.

After the debt is paid in full you will feel good. Rejoice in your accomplishment. Do the same next month and so on. By paying the minimum off first rewards you quicker, so that you get the feeling of accomplishment.

**Invest:** The idea is to have money to invest to reach financial independence. When it comes to investments, you must see what is your yearly expenses that you spend on food and shelter and other sources that is spent on things that don't make money. Start a plan of investing such as the market. Do your researches before you decide what to invest in. Decide how much money you will start with and how much you will be able to invest in the coming years.

**Protect your money:** You must learn to protect your money from others from taking it. That is from lawsuits, government seizures and market fluctuations. Do your research to find out how.

One must get rid of the thought of the scarcity of money. Most of us are taught that money is limited and that there isn't enough to go around. Each fractal division in creation has infinite information of the original source which is infinite. The atom itself is 99.9999 % space and space is filled with energy.

Therefore space is an illusion. Money symbolizes this infinite energy. Money symbolizes life force which comes as resources such as food and other necessities needed to survive. Therefore the limitations on money are what we put on it mentally. Jmmanuel who is known as Jesus said, "Your heart is where your treasure is." That means what you spend your money on is where your heart is. Money is measurement; it measures where your heart is. How many times did one say, "If I had the money I would do such and such," and when they get the money it gets spent elsewhere? That is because one's heart wasn't where they thought it was. Their heart is where the money was spent. Money reveals this about you. If your heart isn't where you want it to be, then that is when you have to step back and reprogram where you want it to be. Money also symbolizes the fertility gods. Since money symbolizes life force it can be used to benefit life or it can be used to bring death. This all depends on the individual who is harnessing this power. When a person is greedy which is basically they are addicted to money, then it brings about the dark side of the fertility which is death. The image of the Grim Reaper is that he holds a scythe. A scythe is a tool that is usually uses to reap crops on a farm. The Grim Reaper image is to reap life. When one is addicted, either one of the two things happen, either the addiction consumes and destroys the individual sparing everyone else, or it destroys everyone else around them before it destroys the individual. Here is the Myth of Midas that gives that example:

Midas was a king of Phrygia, a region nowadays part of Turkey. One day some of his farmhands brought him a satyr they had caught napping in the vineyard. This creature, part man, part goat, still groggy and much the worse for wear, had been thoroughly trussed up to keep him from escaping. Midas immediately recognized Silenus, right-hand satyr to the god Dionysus, and ordered him set free.

Silenus explained that he and his master had just returned from the East where they had been engaged in spreading the cultivation of the grape. Dionysus had brought back a tiger or two, an ever-expanding flock of followers and one very drunken satyr. Silenus had conked out in Midas's vineyard to sleep it off. Now he was grateful to the king for treating him with dignity, and so was Dionysus. The god was so pleased, in fact, that he offered to grant whatever Midas should wish for.

Now, you didn't get to rule a kingdom in those days without a pretty active grasp of what makes for a successful economy. Midas didn't have to think twice. As the simplest plan for the constant replenishment of the royal treasury, he asked that everything he touch be turned to gold.

Arching a godly eyebrow, Dionysus went so far as to ask if Midas were sure. To which the king instantly replied, "Sure I'm sure." So Dionysus waved his pine branch sceptre and conferred the boon.

And Midas rushed back home to try it out. Tentatively at first, he laid a trembling fingertip upon a bowl of fruit and then a stool and then a wooly lambskin. And when each of these had been transmuted in a trice into purest gold, the king began to caper about like the lambkin before its transformation.

"Just look at this!" he crowed, turning his chariot into a glittering mass of priceless-though-worthless transportation. "Look what daddy can do!" he cried, taking his young daughter by the hand to lead her into the garden for a lesson in making dewy nature gleam with a monotonous but more valuable sheen.

Encountering unexpected resistance, he swung about to see why his daughter was being such a slug. Whereupon his eyes encountered, where late his child had been, a life-size golden statue that might have been entitled "Innocence Surprised".

"Uh oh," said Midas, and from that point on the uh-oh's multiplied. He couldn't touch any useful object without it losing in utility what it gained in monetary value, nor any food without it shedding all nutritional potency on its leaden way down his gullet.

This myth showed that due to his greed, he wind up killing his daughter by touching her where she turned into gold. Since he was unable to eat, he would die. Many people misquote and say that, "Money is the root of all evil" the correct saying is, "The love of money is the root of all evil," this is talking about loving money before anything else, like being addicted to a drug. When you use money as a way to benefit lives, there is a lot that you can do that helps you, your love ones and society. It then becomes a force that brings life to all. Just like on George Lucas Star Wars the Jedi and the evil Sith both tap into the same Force. The Jedi uses the Force for good and the Sith uses the Force for evil. Money can ease stress and benefit relationships; it can improve health because you can afford to get the care you want. Through charities, it can be used to help humanity, and if you are making money by providing service, you are also helping people. On the other hand, a drug dealer or thief is making money by destroying life. Drug addicts are buying their poisons, many of those same drug addicts are out committing crimes so that they have the money to buy more of their poisons. Therefore the dealer is adding to the problem to this domino effect. The money that he does make usually doesn't benefit relationships around him. That hidden scarcity mentality that drove him to sell drugs in the first place usually permeates everything else. He is most not likely going to be given as much as the one who legally makes a living who knows that there is no limit to what is flowing out there. The purpose of Tithe is to put the mindset that you are not losing anything because money is limitless. The fear of tithe is indicating that money is limited, so you can't afford to give. Instead of tithe to need, you tithe to abundance in order to bring abundance into your life. Tithing is not charity. It is giving to those who inspire you, reminds you of who you are and lifts you up. This can be any organization or individual. It is whoever gives you that feeling of hope and inspiration.

Above tithe is giving to anyone that you want for any reason. Tithing is the beginning of giving. Tithing is the baby step to giving. Giving beyond tithing is when you are really giving. The more you give, the more you receive. Your confidence in receiving grows as you give. Giving to someone because your motive is to seek something such as approval from that person is not giving. Doing something so someone can do something for you can cause one to feel cheated when that other person doesn't do what you expected. It doesn't give one the confidence that more will come because of the intent and motive. Therefore it isn't the outside appearance that matters, it's the intent. Two different people can give money to someone with two different motives. The one who is giving because they want to and it feels good to give; knowing they are not losing anything will receive more. The one who gives because they have a motive will feel and have regrets when the other doesn't return their favor. How many times some have gave because they found it hard to say "no" as they hope the other will pay them back in some form to just get let down and disappointed while filled with regret because now they are broke? This happens often and this isn't truly giving. Giving in a true sense is knowing that you can afford it and it doesn't matter if you get something back, you just did it because you wanted to. That is given. We are here to emulate the Light. The Light expands and shares. Being a tight-ass isn't emulating the Light. By emulating the Light we allow our vessel to receive more Light. Light comes in many forms, in this case it comes in the form of money. To move past this Power Center is to get rid of scarcity thinking and emulate the Light.

# THE SECOND SPIRAL
## (Element *Water*)

The second spiral of the Power Center is located in the groin area. It is the sacral center. It is associated with the element Water. This Power Center is about sexuality. Here is a correspondent of the symbolism of this power center.

**Element:** Water
**Function:** sexuality, desire, creativity
**Glands:** ovaries, testicles
**Unbalances:** Impotence, frigidity, lower back problems
**Color:** orange
**Sephira:** Yesod

This spiral when plugged in one sees sex in a healthy way. You always make time for your partner to have sex, even if you been with them for many years. You chose the right partners and you are intimate with them. Intimacy means that you can open up to your partner without the fear of them judging you as some type of freak or slut. You also enjoy every moment with them; it isn't just a means to an end to have an orgasm. You feel secured in your relationships.

When the connection of the plug is weak then guilt and shame is associated with sex. When one feels guilt and shame, they also don't like intimacy. The intensity and closeness is uncomfortable. Many put up walls trying to protect themselves from possibly getting hurt. These walls to protect one from being hurt actually make one more vulnerable. This keeps one from making the connections to others as a resource. It keeps one cut of from valuable information. Law 18 in the 48 Laws of Power by Robert Green says "Do Not Build Fortresses to Protect Yourself – Isolation is Dangerous," a fortress seems the safest, but the isolation makes you vulnerable. Connections are important. When you cut yourself off with your connections with others then when you are involved with someone, it's easy to fall into the trap of making that person your whole world even if you have a wall to protect you from that person who is now the center of your world.

Part of life comes from interacting with others. We are social animals. To have success in life, one has to communicate effectively with people. This is by having trust. This is how we get our needs met. Trust is what is needed to have connectedness. When this sacred center is weak, one has trust issues.

The one who you must have connectedness the most with is the God within. Once you have the connection with the God Within then you can feel safe to make connections with others. When this Power Center is not plugged in well one tends to feel that they cannot be loved by being themselves. They find it hard to believe that others can possibly love them. They struggle with seeing themselves as sexy and may experience either premature or delayed ejaculation, they rarely orgasm the same time as their partner.

Sometimes traumatic experiences such as sexual assault may cause us to disconnect by unplugging that sexual Power Center. When we feel guilt or shame in association with sex, then many of us either become fidget or become promiscuous. The promiscuity is a coping mechanism of trying to make sex right because one feels that sex is wrong. While one is promiscuous they lack intimacy. Orgasm is a means to an end. They tend to want to get it over with so that they can get the feeling of the release of the orgasm. Shame just creates obsession. When this energy center is weak, one doesn't like the strong emotions that sex conjures. Fidget people just avoid sex because of this, whereas sex addicts want it to get over with to just chase the orgasm. That is the reason why these addicts mostly settle for bad sex, such as pornography and prostitutes. I am not saying there is nothing wrong with porn, but sex addicts settle for activities that they don't really have to get emotionally attach to. They avoid intimacy so that they will not get hurt.

# The Mother

Every human being has come into this world born out of the womb of their mother. This is an analogy for the origin of all life. The bond between mother and child continues to relate to the individual's relationship with the Divine. The mother is everything to the new born child. To the new born child she is God. She provides everything that the child needs to grow and mature. She is the source of nourishment and abundance. When she does this like she is suppose to, the child develops with a sense of security and trust. It is this sense of security and trust that is needed to be in oneness with the Divine, which is the God within.

All trust issues originate from the mother. Growing up, the father may take a large part in it, but it is up to the mother to protect her child even from the father if he is a danger. He may be able to overpower her, but she has the choice to allow him to continue to be in her and her child's life or not.

Self esteem and self worth is based on the bonding between mother and child. Pleasurable experiences send a message to the child of acceptance and love. On the other hand painful experiences send messages of rejection and insecurity. These messages don't only affect the relationship between mother and child, but also how that child's relationship to his/her own body as well. If the baby is constantly being denied pleasure and being rejected, it will also affect the development of the brain, self esteem and the self worth of the individual. This will cause pleasure and pain to be confused to the point where intimacy will be associated with pain. This subconscious programming of intimacy being related to pain and insecurity will affect the choices of future relationships. This person with this self sabotaging programming will have relationship problems. To protect themselves from the uncomfortable feelings of intimacy they will subconsciously disconnect their second Power Center to the degree that makes them feel comfortable. This is what causes this Power Center to become slightly or more unplugged. When it is unplugged it becomes weak or closed.

On the other hand when the mother and child bonding is healthy, then that child will receive messages of physical acceptance, his/her brain will develop fully, and they will have high self esteem and self worth, while associating pleasure and security with intimacy. He will take delight in all pleasures and see them as inherit rights.

As he/she grows, he/she will see all fulfillments of desires are natural. Achieving goals will be no problem. Since this individual will have feelings of abundance and security he will be able to expand to connecting with others and eventually find a healthy relationship with a mate.

The Earth is also a manifestation of the mother. All plants, animals and us humans are dependent upon the source of Mother Earth. The Earth nourishes us; she is the supporter of our bodies and provides us with abundance from her body.

In the language of Sumer the word AMA meant womb and earth. The Aryan word Mater was used for mother and measurement. From this we get the words matter and metric, matrix and material. The word matrix means womb of matter. Matter is the mirror of the Divine. There is no separation between the Divine and Nature. They are one. The one who has that connection knows there is no separation. They see pleasure of things as inherit gifts. The individual who has a weak energy center at this level tends to get jealous in relationships. Sometimes they can become possessive. When you realize that all is inherit gifts, there is no need for ownership, because one realizes that no one truly owns anything or anyone. Being aware of the God Within, you know that you and all is an extension of the Source. Therefore if all is an extension there is no need to be possessive of anything as you realize all is an extension of you. Realizing this also shows that you have trust which is essential in any healthy relationship.

When it comes to the earth, health of the land and community is important. Fertility of the land always meant wealth and abundance for the community. Anything that prevents the earth from providing food is seen as a lost of wealth, security and life. There is a link between the word economy and ecology. The Greek word oikos which the words come from means house or household. It was understood that for anyone to have a sustainable economy in the house, one had to have a sustainable relationship with the larger household called earth. The Indo-European word for oikos, traces its root to the word weik from where the Anglo-Saxon word Wicca comes from, which today we get the modern word witch. Witches who was female leaders of the clan, was in charge of managing their household economies through their spiritual relationship with the Earth. This was the ultimate source of power and wealth. This bond with Mother Earth, where there is awareness between earth and wealth causes the deep feelings of connectedness, trust and security. One realizes there is a bond between us the earth and all living things upon the earth.

In places where natives live, they have this bonding and when foreigners come in and want to plumage their land for their own selfish reasons, the natives feel just as lost as if a child watched his mother get killed. It is as if their entire world is destroyed. In the movie Avatar you can see this as an example how much the Navi tribe was protective of their forest because of the strong bond that was their whole life.

Another bonding part that is critical that relates to part of the earth is our body. Our mother who nourishes us who is also the beginning of our experiences of pleasure influences our relationship with our body. The formative years are important, if we are being rejected at this time, it can cause lack of development of our brain to the point of not being impaired. Studies have shown that touch stimulation and pleasure is a necessity for the development of the brain. In some cases a child died from being totally rejected from lack of touch. So even if the baby is fed, but if he is totally rejected in everything else, that baby has a high chance of dying from lack of development.

The next stage in growth when the child is nourished properly is when the Divine goes from Universal Mother to mate. This mate leads one to a life transforming place, either as a partner on a physical level or the inner psyche. At this level sexual desire is a asset. In some pagan traditions a man who has sex with a woman who is the incarnate of the Goddess is a hero. The way of the hero is a natural maturity level where he does not fear desire, repress his sexuality nor seek conquest. Conquest is none other than trying to claim ownership. One who is secure enough to stands on their two feet can surrender to the feminine principle of pleasure and desire. He is able to surrender to life. The hero doesn't try to escape life or conquer it, he just lives it fully.

As one surrenders to life, he/she then moves to appreciate the natural order of the Universe, the Laws of Creation. In almost every culture it was believed the Mother Goddess gave the rules of life to mankind. Today the image of Justice is a woman holding a balance of scales. This most likely originates from Egypt from the goddess Maat. At the time of a person's death, Maat would weigh their heart against her feather of truth on the balance scales of Judgment.

The Chinese calls this natural order of the Universe, Tao which means 'The Way.' In Sumer it's called ME and in India it's called Dharma. When one has this interconnectedness they have no need to try to possess or control others. They can just sit back and enjoy life. When you are jealous and controlling, you cannot enjoy life.

The interconnectedness is natural due to the natural bonding with the Divine starting with the bonding of one's mother, then with the lover and a sense of balance with Nature which means the desires are freely in accord with the creative flow of the Universe. The bonding of the mother automatically causes one to be in tuned with the God Within. The lover internally is the anima which is the feminine principle of the soul in man. In women the male principle is the animus. This internal lover automatically happens due to the self esteem and self worth one feels due to their mother's bonding. Sometimes we find that counterpart of the soul in a physical partner that completes us.

If the early bonding between mother and child is weak, that individual's sense of self is injured. The addictions to sex, food, drugs and even money are a rooted to this lack of our bonding to our mother. When you have a world full of people who had mother bonding issues, you get dysfunctional people who has low self worth who has to boost up their self esteem through drug use or controlling others or greed for monetary power. The world would be a better place to live in if not for these issues. All the problems in the world first originate in our homes.

The reason why Adultery and fornication was included in the laws of the commandments is because thousands of years ago men while traveling would impregnate women and leave them left alone. Many women were unable to handle raising a child by themselves. This would interfere with the woman's life due to the father's lack of responsibility. I am not saying unmarried sex is wrong, I am just explaining why it was included in these laws due to these factors. Today we have contraceptives and can have responsible sex with partners. Unfortunate you still have men today who are just as irresponsible. Not only does this behavior interfere with the life of the woman, it can strongly affect the child.

Bonding is very critical in the formative years. If the mother of the child is overwhelmed because they can't handle raising a child on their own, it affects the child. This feeling of being overwhelmed can hinder the bonding process needed if the mother is holding some hidden suppressed resentment about her situation. If that child senses this resentment he/she will feel some type of rejection. The child may feel that his mother is just going through the motions, just like when someone hugs us, we can sense if the hug is genuine or fake even when the motions are the same. These actions just create a domino effect. If the child lacks the bonding, he/she may grow up and chose an unhealthy relationship and have a child that just grows up to continue the pattern. During this domino effect you have generations of children who are drug addicts, rapists, murderers, and money grubbers, all the ingredients to keep the world in a dysfunctional state. Therefore man and woman should either have responsible sex or if they decide to have a child, to make sure they are economically fit where one can relax and fully commit to the raising of the child. Take the lesson from the wolves. When a wolf meets their mate, they are compatible before they take the next step. Through hunting the wolves make sure they have plenty of food before they have pups. When these pups are born, there are no worries about if there is enough to feed their offspring. Without these worries, the pups can have their mother's undivided attention while the bonding is strong between mother and pups.

Humans here on this earth tend to do things backwards. Many couples find out after marriage they are not compatible. They have a child while struggling with financial problems. Once you have a child before you're economically stable it's almost impossible to become economically stable afterwards. When both parents are worried about if they will have enough to provide for the family, one cannot give their undivided attention that is needed for the child.

In the Pleiades the parents don't see their children as their own property, therefore once the original bonding takes place, love and attention is given to all children from the community. The newly born are emotionally and mentally protected by any negative influences until they reach the stage where they can learn to think and understand themselves well enough to deal with it. Too often children here on earth are not protected by negative influences due to those influences right there in the home. It is unhealthy to argue in front of children, this automatically causes the child to think it's because of him/her.

In the Pleiades according to many sources, the first ten years are spent on education of learning who they are. The children then become secured and well-balanced within themselves. If a woman does become pregnant and she weighs out the situation and realizes right now isn't the best time, she will get an abortion

26

before the fetus develops and wait at a later time to give birth where she can put all her energy into bringing a mentally healthy child into the world. According to Meir the Pleiadians have up to the first three weeks to decided, after the 21$^{st}$ day it is too late to get an abortion. She knows if she brings a child into the world where she won't be able to be fully devoted, that child can become unstable and develop with self-esteem and self image problems. If ones creativity is denied then this same energy is unnaturally expressed in destructive ways.

Even studies show that when animals are denied physical pleasure the results lead to cruelty and aggression. When one is secured and well-balanced, then they take on the characteristics of compassion, caring, empathy and affection. One in this natural stage sees that every life is a piece of the whole. To harm any life on this interconnected web is to harm all even ourselves. Together we are God, together we are one. This is the reason why our elder brothers and sisters from other worlds come here to teach and guide us. They see that we are all one and what happens to us here affects all.

As we see how this all connects together. First the bonding with the Divine as the nurturing mother, then as one matures the Divine comes as the lover. Within this whole framework, one develops a sense of security and trust, then one easily enjoy the fulfillment of desires, where one develops self esteem and personal power and one sees the interconnectedness and have compassion for all life, then through all of it, one enjoys freedom.

Long time ago man was at the hunting and gathering stage, once we reach the agricultural stage our views changed. We then were able to have time to do other things in life. People were able to explore other things in life and indulge and live life to the fullest. This is the root motivation of all human beings and it is the creative energy given rise to all cultures.

When a child is secured emotionally his/her creative energy is released. A child who is secured will not be concerned with sleep, food or anything else, while he /she is playing. The child would be totally absorbed in play. While in play the child is exploring, learning and discovering. While the child is playing he/she is filled with joy. This is what life should be about. 'All work and no play make jack a dull boy.' Life is about having fun while you are learning, discovering and creating. The spiritually evolved integrates his creative play to the point where he creates things that are unique that he gives to the world.

When the Divine is seen as the lover, then our creative sex drive frees the creative energies of the spirit in one's life. The sex drive in humans is stronger than it is in any other animal. The creativity released is strong enough to birth a civilization or a masterpiece. The Divine expresses itself through sexual creative energies that transcend boundaries.

This Power Center is associated with the element water. From water all life begins. This center corresponds with bodily fluids such as blood, semen, ova and other bodily secretions.

On the Tree of Life it is associated with Yesod which is the sphere of water and the moon. The moon has a pull on water causing tidal waves. It also effects our emotions due to its effects on our blood. The moon even effects the time of menstruation.

Blood was used in early times as a symbol in all religious rituals. Cavemen used red ochre to symbolize the red blood of Mother Earth in burial ceremonies. Red ochre was also used in the cave walls and on statues of the Mother Goddess. Some cultures such as the Austrian aborigines rub menstrual blood on their bodies and their sacred stones. Menstrual blood was believed to have powers of regeneration and creation.

When a girl was in the phase of becoming a woman her menstrual blood was her sign. It was believed that her blood had magical powers and was life itself. Menstrual blood was also use to fertilize the earth. Agriculture rested upon the bond between blood and soil.

The menstrual blood was a symbol of great spiritual power. Menstrual blood was also symbolized rebirth. In ancient times one would paint themselves in menstrual blood as they believed it would have a more abundant life and afterlife.

There was a strong bond between Mother Goddess and blood. In later years when cultures incorporated the Male God there also had to be a blood bond as well, the problem is men don't shed blood like women, so they had to mutilate their penises. Circumcision among the Hebrews was considered a "sign of the covenant" between God and his people. Male Gods also had to bond with the blood from the womb to achieve power. The god Thor for example gained Immortality by bathing in menstrual blood. Post menopausal woman were believed to be all wise and powerful.

Kings were anointed with the Queen's menstrual blood to gain wisdom and power. In Tantra the goddess must be menstruating when she has sex with her male partner, so that the God will share in her power. In ancient times man could not own land, he would have to be married for that to happen. Through matrimony a man can bond through a ritual with a woman and then claim ownership of the land. Matrimony means to inherit property of the Matre (Mother).

As the concept of mediator developed the idea of savior making sacrifice of blood was born. This is seen in such deities as Dionysus and Jesus. In the Church the ritual is symbolizes as wine to symbolize the blood of the savior. In these rituals those who drink the blood are united with the savior as a promise of immortality. The word yoga means yoke which is union. It is to have union with the base self and higher self.

To plug in this Power Center is to drink in the sweet waters of pleasure. The spiritual science to do this is Tantra. The word Tantra comes from the word (tan) means profound matters relating to the principles of reality and (tra) means to liberate. Therefore Tantra is a continuing creative process of integration that leads to an ever expanding of consciousness. By unifying the two polarities within the totality of the mind, the consciousness starts to expand. This is the Sacred Marriage within. The symbol of the Sacred Marriage is two intertwined snakes in union around the Tree of Life. In Egypt it is the staff of Tehuti. The serpent that symbolizes the cool lunar pole is Nekhebet and the warm solar pole Uadjit. These are two goddesses with opposite poles. In India it's the goddess and god Ida and Pingala. Today the staff of Tehuti is the caduceus (figure 2.1). These are the two poles of the Life Force in the body. It can be seen as male and female since solar is usually a male symbol in many cultures. The caduceus symbol is the medical health symbol seen often today.

Figure 2.1
Medical caduceus

The Serpent Power force rises from the base of the spine when aroused and passes through each Power Center and reaches the crown Power Center and reaches oneness. That oneness is enlightenment or Illumination. In the book 'Coming Forth by Day Uadjit/Uatchet is the destroyer of evil forces that try to subdue the initiate. You may notice you breathe out of one nostril more than the other. One nostril breathes the solar and the other the lunar.

The symbol of the Sacred Marriage became the most powerful symbol in human consciousness. The inner god and inner goddess within each human through sexual union of the Sacred Marriage will unite in ecstasy.

Tantra sees that all matter is energy and all energy is a manifestation of Consciousness. Breathe is the link between body and consciousness. Breathe is our direct experiences with Life Force. Notice that when you are stressed, you will find your breathing shallow. Be aware of your breathing connects you to your body. Being aware of how energy moves in your body is the first step in the practice of Tantra.

Some traditions say sexual energy is not sacred as other energies. The thing is that all energy within and without the body is sacred. Lust is an asset, many traditions say do not have lust in your heart when you work on Tantra. Lust is the desire that gave birth to life. You were born by lust; therefore lust cannot be of a lesser if it was the spark that gave birth to humanity. Religions had frown down upon lust due to seeing the body as less value. How many times have you heard preachers talk about the sins of the flesh? They want to see that flesh is a bad thing because it connects us to our animal nature. This is how the powers to be try to separate us from nature. Many people today struggle with shame due to the taboos forced upon us.

# Taboos

We live in a world with so many taboos. The thing is we are designed to want what we can't have. Therefore a taboo is something that we are told is forbidden. When something is taboo, it causes us to want it more. If sex and walking around naked was NOT taboo, pornography would not be interesting. Porn sells because of the taboos placed upon sex. The more forbidden, the more attractive it becomes. Write down sexual taboos that turn you on but may feel shame about.

_____

_____

_____

**Intimacy:** We all have sexual fantasies that we keep mostly to ourselves. We secretly want to indulge in, but we are afraid to tell our partner due to the fear that she/he will judge us as a nasty freak or slut. Because of this shame with taboo, we never get our sexual needs totally fulfilled. Many turn to prostitutes because they are too ashamed to tell their partner what they want. They may feel safer to tell the prostitute because they don't care what the prostitute thinks. To improve your sex life, it is important to tell your partner your sexual needs and fantasies. You may be just as surprise if she opens to you and share her fantasies. You may come to realize there was no need to have shame for your fantasy when you come to realize that her fantasies aren't all that much different. The shame is due to us thinking that we are all alone in thinking the way we do, so we question ourselves if something is wrong with us.

There is nothing wrong with acting out any sexual fantasy at all as long as all those participating are consenting adults. Two words, consenting and adults only.

Some of us have deep sexual fears. There are reasons why we have these fears. Perhaps something traumatic happened to cause the fears. Perhaps it could be a hidden desire that we want to repress. For example some people are homophobic and many times it's because that individual is struggling inside about their own denial of attraction to the same sex. Homophobic that attack homosexuals are doing that to take the attention away from what's going on inside themselves. Whatever you sexual fears are write them down.

---

---

---

After writing them down, observe and ask yourself why you have these fears. This time make a four column list. Here is an example below.

| Sexual fears | Automatic thoughts | Reasons why | Letting go (acceptance) |
|---|---|---|---|
| Homosexuals make me uncomfortable | Goodgirls don't have sex with women, to do so would make one less of a woman and a pathetic sinner. | Church raised me to believe it is wrong.<br><br>I feel like something wrong with me, because I am a woman attracted to women.<br><br>I am afraid what others will think of me. | Could the church be wrong? Maybe that is just between me and God.<br><br>Perhaps accepting that I like women, is accepting who I am and it doesn't make me less than a woman. |

This is one example. You write whatever your issue may be, maybe. Maybe you are a guy who is secretly attracted to large women and ashamed because you are worried what others may think. Due to this, one will not be content if they are choosing thin woman when they are really attracted to obese women. The same with someone who is homosexual, they will not be happy if they are choosing the opposite sex for appearance. To be content, one has to accept what they like without worrying about what others think.

What makes us who we are is every part of us. If you are baking a cake for example, it takes many ingredients. If it's a lemon cake, the ingredients will contain butter, eggs, sugar, lemon, milk, vanilla extract and flour. Some of these ingredients may not sound pleasant alone, maybe even bitter, but all are necessary to make this lemon cake. The same goes with us, those aspects of ourselves that we consider faults are part of the ingredients that make us who we are, and must be accepted.

## Abusive relationships

Many times we see a pattern in our relationships. Each relationship we jump into it's the same old BS. Same mess with a different name and face. Some just jump to the conclusion that all men or all women are the same. That isn't the case; it's the pattern that one is choosing. As I said earlier, it all starts from the degree of bonding we have with our mother. For example, we are not getting the nurturance from our mother we already feel rejection and associate intimacy with pain, if our daddy is abusive on top of that; all this becomes a subconscious comfort zone. What happens is that when we get older we subconsciously attract partners that fit our comfort zone. This person who lacks unavailability from their mother and abuse by their father will tend to pick partners who are unavailable and abusive. Write down the pattern of abuse that you have been experiencing in your relationships.

---

---

---

Now that you are aware of this pattern, write down what pattern you see in your relationships that you can relate to growing up at home with your parents. Were your parents unavailable? Was either one abusive? Perhaps your mother wasn't available because she had a drinking problem, perhaps your father was abusive because he was abused and taught that is what is to be done, or he had his own issues on control. Realizing this, makes you realize that it's not all about you. They had their own hang-ups and now as an adult you have the power to make the changes to what you want. You have the power to nurture your needs what you may have not received from your mother bonding. Now make a list of the traits that you want in a romantic relationship. What do you want in your partner?

_____

_____

_____

Remember water seeks its own level. What is it that you need to work on yourself? Perhaps there is some inner work you need to work on to have this relationship that you just written down. Write down what you think you need to work on to have the relationship that you want.

_____

_____

_____

Many times when we are hurt in a relationship we tend to focus on what they did to us. Focusing on this just sets you up to continue the pattern. We attract what we think about the most. When you think about what harm someone did, you are thinking about them. Thinking about them will either attract them back into your life, or you will attract someone else that is very much like them. Healing is necessary to stop the pattern of choosing bad relationships. Shifting our thoughts may be one of the main things that we needed to do to make those changes within. Become aware of your thoughts and shift your thoughts as much as possible to what you want out of the relationship. Avoid jumping into another relationship right away. Many of us have this habit of doing this. Allowing yourself time to heal gives you the strength not to be needy or desperate as you feel that you alone can stand on your own two feet. It is this feeling of security that is needed to have better judgment to make better choices. Given yourself time and focusing on what you want in a relationship will eventually open the door when you are ready to receive it.

## Tantra

There are techniques that can help you heal. Tantra can help you receive the nurturance and pleasure that you deserve so that you can have that freedom. Freedom to enjoy life to the fullest. Increasing energy in the brain will cause your consciousness to expand and increase your awareness. Yoga typically is associated with asceticism and perfection. Many teachers have put their own personal issues into the philosophy. For example, sex addiction wasn't known until recent years, though sex addiction has existed since humans existed and create taboos concerning sex. Those teachers who may have struggled with sex addiction not realizing the addiction is the problem, not sex itself, would come to the conclusion that complete abstinence is the key. Any addiction, no matter what it is depletes energy and devalues the self. These teachers that don't realize they are addicted, so therefore they come to the conclusion that sex devalues them and depletes energy. When they exercise willpower to choose abstinence they feel more whole and don't realize the exercising of willpower alone is what made them feel better, they then instead come to the conclusion that lack of sex made them feels whole. They then write doctrines that abstinence is the key and by not having an orgasm you maintain more energy and live longer. Every addiction a teacher may have struggled with without realizing what's going on came up with a new doctrine to add to the doctrine of asceticism for all followers to follow. Originally Tantra yoga is not about perfection, it's about being fully who you are. When it comes to sex, having a sexual orgasm at least once a week is healthy. The idea of Tantra is to create the union of the male and female within, the anima and animus of the psyche. When you exercise the will which spins the back of the vortex counterclockwise, whereas the feelings generated from the will spin the other half of the vortex in the front clockwise. Here is a diagram (Figure 2.2) of the Power Centers that are vortexes.

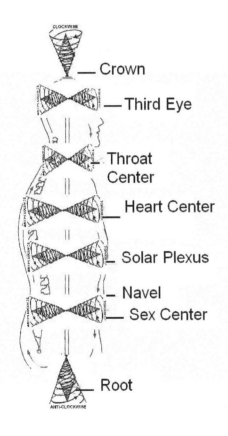

— Crown

— Third Eye

— Throat Center

— Heart Center

— Solar Plexus

— Navel

— Sex Center

— Root

Figure 2.2
Spiraling vortex centers

Life Force is everywhere. It moves within our body. The Chinese call it Chi, the Japanese its Ki and in India it's called Prana. When we breathe it moves from the base of the spine up the back as we inhale. When we exhale the Life Force travels back down the spine. The polarity that moves up is the lunar or female polarity. The polarity that moves down is the solar male polarity.

Conscious movement of Life Force is the whole technology of Tantra yoga. As I said earlier by becoming aware of your breath, you become aware of your body. Due to trauma or rejection that causes pain, we escape the pain by becoming numb to our awareness as a way to protect ourselves from being hurt.

## Uatchet and Nekhebet

The two current poles moving through the spine is negative and positive poles. The negative pole is the lunar which Nekhebet symbolizes. The positive pole is the solar which Uatchet symbolizes. The lunar energy (Nekhebet) is cooling, it starts from the base of the spine, moves up to top of head and comes down through the brain and through the forehead and out of the left nostril.

The current that moves downward, the solar (Uatchet) is warm and begins at the right nostril and moves up the forehead into the brain, then descends down the spine to the base. (see Figure 2.3)

This current is what keeps us alive; the idea of Tantra is to increase this. Through sexual union the energy can be increased in the body until it reaches orgasm. This increase in energy in the brain expands consciousness due to neurons in the brain being stimulated.

Just like in Creation, the desire of the Source creates a disturbance in the vacuum of space, from that comes positive (father) and negative (mother) ions. These two poles of ions come together as electricity. Electricity is the offspring of both poles of ions. Electricity creates a disturbance and eventually from this stimulation comes the birth of the atom, from that comes the manifestation of all material bodies. The union between mothers and fathers are always giving birth. The current in our spine, that union creates expanded consciousness which is called by names such as Cosmic Consciousness or Christ Consciousness.

Figure 2.3
Circulation of Uatchet and Nekhebet

Some of these exercises involve touching and nurturance. Receiving nurturance is the first step that way we are then able to give nurturance to others.

First drink a large glass of water and feel it pour inside you. Feel the coolness of the water; feel the wetness of the water as it goes down. Take a wet finger and rub your face, feeling the cool wetness. Next step is to clean yourself with water. This ritual cleansing should be pleasurable. You can choose any form of cleansing you enjoy.

Next step is to do an exercise called the cobra. (Figure 2.4) This exercise will strengthen the back and abdomen muscles. Digestion is also stimulated and the body becomes alive with energy as the chest opens and breath expands.

Lay face down with palms face flat on the floor next to the chest. Have the elbows close to the body and have your toes and heels together.

Inhale and lengthen the whole body. Lift your head up as you expand the chest forward. Relax the shoulder blades down the back while lifting mostly with the back and neck your pelvis remains on the floor.

Rise up the most that you can while remaining comfortable. Be aware of your lower back as you look upward in a 45 degree angle.

Breathe evenly and deeply, inhale while rising and exhale while settling. Hold the pose as long as comfortable. When you release, exhale and then lay flat with your head to the side. Relax and lay there for a minute.

The next exercise is the locust posture (Figure 2.5). While lying on your belly stretch out your feet pressing against the floor, make sure your arms are pressed down on the sides. First time doing this, raise just one leg up as far as you can and hold for 30 seconds then released. Then put it down slowly and do the same with the other leg. When advanced then raise both your thighs up to the ceiling and firm your legs. Move your tailbone in the direction of your heels while keeping pelvis pressed against the floor.

Figure 2.4
Cobra Posture

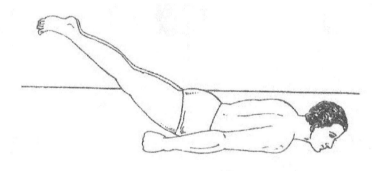

Figure 2.5
Locust

**Alternate nostril breathing:** The opposite energy poles in the body, Nekhebet and Uatchet can be balanced through alternate nostril breathing. The lunar breath in left nostril is cooling to the body. The solar breath is heating to the body. Solar breath is useful when physical activity is needed, as well as to heat the body to fight illnesses. During an illness the left nostril should be blocked off to heat up the body. This happens automatically sometimes when we have a cold. Lying on the left side at bedtime will cause you to breathe more through the right nostril.

To do this takes your right hand, bend index finger leaving the thumb and pinky free. Use the thumb to close off the right nostril and inhale through the left nostril. Then close both nostrils release the thumb from right nostril and exhale through the right nostril while left one is held closed. Do this for a few minutes alternating.

**Meditation for integration:** This exercise is for alternate nostril breathing, to balance the negative and positive polarities in the body. Visualize yourself gaining cosmic energy. Feel it accumulate in the body. Inhale and visualize the energy flowing up from the base through each vortex. Hold the breath a few seconds upon exhaling feel the energy go back down.

Sexual union between opposite poles creates the birth of what can be called the magical child. That magical child is consciousness expansion. In Ancient India they had art in mythology that described this union. (Figure 2.6). All   Tantra doesn't require a partner. Some forms can also be solitary for we all have both female and male polarities within.

Figure 2.6
Tantra Indian Art

**Sexercise:** There are preparation exercises. One is to contract the anal sphincter muscles repeatedly you would tighten those muscles as if you was preventing yourself from having a bowel movement. This not only strengthens the pelvic muscles, but will also increase energy at the root center for the purpose of orgasm without ejaculation. Do this at least 10 repetitions. Then relax and draw the lunar energy up the spine upon inhalation. Touch the tongue to the roof of your mouth ( this completes the circuit) and hold it there for 5 seconds. Then exhale allowing the energy to go back down the spine. Do this routine all over again at least 5 times. Do this for about a week before the next exercise.

The next exercise would be to contract the urethra sphincter muscles. This is the muscles used to stop yourself from peeing. Try stopping the flow of urine while peeing to get a feel for it. These muscles are located under the clitoris of women and at the base of the penis in men. In women if she put her fingers inside herself, she should be able to feel the muscles slightly squeezing her fingers. Not only will this strengthen muscles where one can hold their urine better, but for men it will stimulate the genitals and increase energy. Keep an erection longer and may help cure impotence. Women it will help with child birth, increase sensitivity in the clitoris and increase orgasm. This will also cause you to be able to have longer orgasm.

With this exercise do the same as previous exercise. 10 repetitions, touch tongue to roof, hold for 5 seconds, and draw energy up upon inhale and exhale letting energy flow downward. Repeat 5 times for a week.

**Divine Lover:** make sure that your environment is aesthetically pleasing. Have flowers, candles or whatever that will put you in an erotic mood. Prepare the room for love; make it something special since you are inviting your Divine Lover.

Sit and meditate comfortably. Make sure your spine is straight. While sitting in meditative positions start to stimulate yourself. You can use pictures to enhance if you wish. Let your hands become your Divine Lover.

**Masturbation:** Masturbation can be used for transformation. Masturbation can give you insight on how your body works sexually and energetically. Those who suffer from a sexual dysfunction can use self pleasure as a way to self treatment. Self stimulation also enhances sexual health. Sexual arousal and orgasm causes beneficial hormones that are released in the blood stream. These hormones can improve your mood as it releases stress.

Many people are inhibited by their fantasies due to shame. Can you fantasize about other people outside your partner, or is that cheating? Is it ok to fantasize about being a sadist or is that being a sicko? Another concern people have is fantasizing is putting energy into having it manifest. Have fun with your fantasies. If you want to fantasies about having sex with monsters, animals and dark strangers in the night, then fantasize. If you do not want the fantasy to happen in real life then it will not manifest. Fantasies are harmless as long as you can tell the difference between fantasy and reality. Fantasy is a way to explore other realities and can be fun, like I said earlier when the fantasy is repressed, it leads to obsession.

**Extended Orgasm:** Stimulate yourself until you are about to reach orgasm. Before you do stop and breathe slowly and deeply until the desire to orgasm fades. Repeat a few times, each time when you getting close, pull back.

**Empathy sex:** During masturbation fantasize about your lover. Imagine that you are the person you fantasizing about. Feel how you feel to the other person, and then imagine that you are both you and your partner at once. This exercise will allow you to perceive how you have orgasm and how you relate to your partner. Be in the moment. Enjoy every pleasure that you are experiencing at the moment. Feel every part of the senses that you are experiencing. Allow yourself to be carried away with all the pleasures and emotions that are coming to surface.

**Breathing and Orgasm:** When you come to an orgasm, test with different sorts of breathing. See what happens when you breathe slow and deep. Hard or fast. What happens when you moan? Experiment.

**Extended Orgasm:** As you continue to stimulate yourself very slowly and steady. Continue to imagine that you are with your lover. Breathe deeply until you come close to orgasm. Stop and slow your breathing down until the urge to orgasm has faded some. Draw the energy up the spine. Then masturbate gently to the point of coming close to orgasm again. Do it again at least 5 times. Extended arousal will flood your bloodstream with testosterone and estrogen which stimulate the pineal gland which is associated with the Third eye. This will cause the pineal gland to produce a chemical called methoxyharmalan which is similar to psilocybin which is found in some mushrooms. Your threshold of pleasure will actually increase.

Now this time as you come close to orgasm contract the sphincter muscles at the same time you inhale stand up as you clinch your fist while tongue touches the roof of your mouth while you roll your eyes up into your skull. Make sure that you have some cushion behind you. This energy of the orgasm goes straight into your head and it may make you become unconscious for a second, enough time to cause you to fall backwards.

Now stimulate yourself and pull the energy to the solar plexus, pull back and start again, this time to the heart center and pull back and stimulate again by pulling energy to the head area then release and have fun spilling your seed if that's what you desire.

If you decide to have a partner, learn to build this energy by sharing it with your partner. You can learn to pass this energy back and forth in your lover. Some traditions see the blending of the sexual fluids as sacred. The Gnostic Catholic Church which is part of the Ordo Templis Orientis baked Cakes of Light which have the mixture of both male and female fluids from copulating after Tantra inside the cakes that is used for Communion.

Have you ever notice why you can tell a genuine hug from someone who is just going through the motions? That is because during a hug there is an exchange of energy taking place. On a subconscious level agreement is made on who is receiving and who is giving the energy. Receiving is the female polarity, but one doesn't have to be a female to receive. It doesn't matter what gender, both agree subconsciously what roles are being played during this exchange of energy. Even though this happens on a subconscious level, this exchange can be done consciously. The Pleiadians see sexual energy as a form of communication. They are very intimate and sexual energy flows freely through them. It flows in every aspect of life. Sex is not compartmentalized like it is here on earth.

The Creation which many call God itself is constantly having sex. The desire of God is constantly impregnating the vacuum of space that gives birth to material bodies that give birth to other material bodies. This sex process is unending, things are always being created.

**Energy sharing:** Sit facing your partner. It doesn't matter where you sit. Hold your arms out in front of you with your right palm down and your left palm up. Have your partner do the same as you place your palms on your lover's palms.

Feel the energy flow down your right arm and out the palm of your right palm into the left palm of your lover. Now feel the energy from your partner enter into your left palm. Feel it traveling up the arm, across the shoulders and back down your right arm. Have your partner do the same.

This can be increased by breathing in synch. Once you have practice and mastered this, you can practice it during sex.

Even though the vagina is the geometric gateway to the Cosmos, one doesn't have to have a partner and if one chooses a partner, it doesn't have to be a member of the opposite sex. Within all of us as I said, we have both polarities. Your sexual energy is the Life Force that manifests all things. Your body is your temple where you can through sex have communion with the All That Is.

Pleiadian Spirals of Light

# THE THIRD SPIRAL
## (Element *Fire*)

The third spiral of the Power Center is located in the solar plexus. It is the personal power center. It is associated with the element Fire. It is the seat of emotions. Here is a correspondent of the symbolism of this power center.

**Element:** Fire
**Function:** Will, assertiveness, personal power
**Glands:** Pancreas, adrenals
**Unbalances:** Acid reflex, diabetes, digestion problems
**Color:** yellow
**Sephira:** Hod, Netzach

When this power center is plugged in one has confidence and healthy self-esteem in life and career. You master your emotions instead of being mastered by them. One comes to realize that emotions are just experiences.

When this energy center is weak one identifies with their emotions. One sees themselves as a victim as they blame others for their own mishaps. Since this is the area of "gut feeling" it then becomes blocked and causes one to have a poor judge of character. These people lack discernment and make poor choices. They also are a slave to their emotions. The way to master emotions is to exercise the will.

# Will

We are led to believe that we have free will. The fact is most of us are just reacting to our chemical stimuli and events in our lives. Most of our lives are just swayed by circumstances like a tree branch moving in the wind. We are addicted to the chemical stimuli that produce those feelings that are our comfort zone. This makes us a slave to our emotions. This means that we don't have free will. Free will must be earned. The only way to earn our will is to exercise our will. It must be exercised in order for our feelings to give birth to manifestation. An old Egyptian proverb says "Emotions are good servants but poor masters." Most of us allow our emotions to be our masters. The idea is to exercise the will so that our emotions can be our servants and gives us what we desire.

In each of our Power Centers is a vortex which is two spiraling cones. The spiraling cone in the backside of the body represents the will. When we exercise the will it moves from the back and impregnates the front side of the spiraling cone which is our feelings. Newton's third law of motion is, "for every action there is an equal and opposite reaction." If you throw a basketball at a wall it will bounce back with equal force. The harder you throw it, the harder it bounces back. Emotions are like the basketball. Whatever feelings that you feed, the vibrations from those feelings project out and bounce back in the manifestation of circumstances. If we are stressed and focusing on what we don't want, those feelings will bring circumstance of that which we focus on that we don't want to manifest more. When we are slave to our emotions we are on autopilot. Those automatic thoughts bring feelings that are associated with our automatic thoughts. If we are not aware of those automatic thoughts we then feel emotions that are not pleasant and then we don't know why we feel that way. We become clueless to as why our life is not where we want it to be. Many don't know that their life is in dismay because of their automatic thoughts that creates the vibration that brings the unwanted circumstances in their life. To make these changes, one must first be vigilant and cautious when our automatic thoughts come to us. If you try to fight the unwanted automatic thoughts, you will only feed them. Therefore just acknowledge them and then exercise the will to think of what we do want. This takes conscious effort. When it comes to exercising our will we will have challenges to face. See these challenges as opportunities to grow. In life many have this concept of good versus evil. The definition of evil is that which impedes human evolution. This is based on perception. Circumstances only impede human growth when you allow it to. If you do not allow it to, it will aid in your growth, therefore it isn't evil. Evil is an illusion created by perception. I am not condoning the acts of people who do heinous crimes against humanity. Everything balances itself. Those who do such acts walk in ignorance. They cannot see the Light, for a veil is covered before their eyes. There is a formula for achieving our goals. That formula is:

Desire -------resistance ------- goals
Desire ------ resistance (material world) ---- fulfillment

To achieve a goal we must have desire. The stronger the desire the faster you achieve your goal. We live in a material world and it is designed so that we can grow through resistance. The resistance is challenges and opportunities for growth. Many people see the challenges as problems that they dread. They tend to let the challenges they see as problems that deter them from achieving their goals. One must realize that resistance is an opportunity and that is why we live in a material world. The material world is the whole creation and is the mirror of the Source that many call God. Resistance is necessary for growth. The shell of a chicken egg which protects the embryo must at a certain time be destroyed or the chick will be stifled and its further growth and development made impossible.

Therefore resistance is necessary and those who believe in the duality of good and evil perceive resistance as evil. The two contradicting beliefs that religious doctrine has when it comes to good and evil is:

One: The belief that the world was created by a Being that is all powerful, all knowing and all good and always remained under His guidance.

Two: The belief that evil is not just an illusion, but a power existing independently of good.

This conflict of good and evil has deeply affected the thoughts, ideals, and social customs of humanity, though it can be simply explained.

Good for each of us, is our accomplishment of our own law that brings happiness. Evil is that which opposes it. Every individual has only one law, which is the Law of Good, which is One. The accomplishment of this one Law is Truth. People have within themselves the ability to grasp the power of good and defend themselves from what seems evil. Being created in the center of good they appointed an ideal life free from misunderstanding. By believing that they no longer within that center of good, they experience its absence, which they call evil. People will continue to be punished and harassed by seeming evil until they learn to recognize that evil comes from their own lack of will, which is being a slave to their own impulsiveness to react to resistance. Reacting to resistance would be the passive or aggressive or both approach. Being proactive would be the assertive approach to resistance which causes growth and happiness. Therefore good and evil are just terms for the positive and negative aspects of the same force. We choose how to respond to any external influences that come our way. Victimization for example does not come from what happens to us, but being a victim is how you respond to any situation. If a mugger comes by and snatches your purse, from general terms by the laws of the land, that makes you a victim, but you are not truly a victim if you rise up and assertively handle the situation. That would be going to the authorities and learn and grow from the situation so that you take measures that it doesn't happen again. The one with victim mentality will allow that situation to deter their happiness where one wallows in their self pity without even taking measures to prevent future encounters. While they feel worthless they are unknowingly setting themselves up for future encounters. The next culprit doesn't even have to be the same person.

Therefore we must nurse the thoughts that correspond to the feelings that we want to generate. Our automatic thoughts automatically generate feelings that are associated with them. Many times the feelings that we generate are not the feelings we want. Many of the automatic thoughts manifest anxiety and depression. We tend to become slaves to our unwanted emotions and many of us do not know what to do. Most of us allow our emotions to control us while we run impulsively on autopilot.

What is it that keeps most of us from exercising our will? The answer is pain. We tend to avoid pain and seek pleasure. Humans are prone to seek instant pleasure. Most of us don't want to endure the pain of patience. Patience is the key to success. All things go through a process. Gravity generates electricity and creates a disturbance in the vacuum. Overtime the atom of hydrogen that has one proton manifest. As atoms of hydrogen gather together and cause friction, in time the atom helium that has two protons manifest. This is an ongoing process as each group of atoms manifested has an extra proton than the group previous. From this all atoms are manifested and certain atoms marry other atoms to create molecules. From this everything that exists has manifested. All this took a long process of what we would measure as billions and billions of years. A butterfly had to go through a process. Nothing skips steps; all must go through a cycle of steps. This also applies to us, the key is patience. The way to endure patience is to enjoy the moment.

If you can, go on a trip and instead of anticipating that you can't wait to get there, enjoy what's right in front of you. While on this trip, observe the beauty around you. What do you see? Enjoy the scenery. How is the landscape? Are there mountains and trees? Are there nice houses that you see along the way? Enjoy what it is that you observe.

When it comes to exercising, what is your goal? Are you exercising to lose weight? Are you lifting weights to get muscles? If so, instead of focusing on the end goal, enjoy the moment. How do you feel in the moment of exercising? Do you feel invigorating? Do you feel pleasure of well being? Write down what you like and feel in the moment.

_____

_____

_____

Make a list of these things and remind yourself this immediate pleasure that you feel while you are working out.

_____

_____

_____

If you're just seeking the end result and not enjoying the moment, you most likely will get discouraged. Many people exercise and go on a diet just to lose weight. While exercising they just long for the end result and when they don't see results fast enough, they get discourage and quit. Therefore the idea is to exercise and enjoy the immediate pleasures that you receive from working out. The losing weight should be just the bonus. Don't let exercise just be a means to an end.

The musical artist Madonna said she use to anticipate too finish each album that she created. Now she learned from her practices of Kabbalah to enjoy each moment while she is creating her songs for her albums. Be as a child and learn to play. Enjoy each moment towards your journey.

The idea is to strengthen your will. That means to do something challenging that will benefit your life. If it doesn't benefit your life, there is no need for it. Exercise for example is something that will benefit your life. As you enjoy the immediate pleasure from exercise, also learn to deal with the pain and see the pain as an opportunity to strengthen the will. As your will strengthens your inner vision becomes clearer. This clear vision is you becoming more aware of the God within. This is the eye of God within you

54

opening allowing you to see. Those who cannot see walk in darkness; they are blind to the Light of All That Is. The more reactive we become, the more obscured our vision becomes. This is why the more we become slaves to our emotions, the more feeling of hopelessness we experience. Impulsiveness just obscures our vision. Those who walk totally in darkness, we categorize them as evil. They are just misled and lost individuals.

We must remind ourselves why we are doing something that needs to be done. Each day have a task that will bring you benefits. Get through the pain and do it. One of the benefits of exercising the will is freeing the mind of clutter. This is a form of Mindfulness Meditation. Mindfulness Meditation is focusing on one thought without distraction. I am using willpower to write this book, each day I write a few pages, some days more than others. I keep doing this until my book is finished.

Studies also shown that by strengthening the will you strengthen the prefrontal cortex of the brain, which control the emotional responses which means that you are better fit to handle stress and less prone to impulsiveness.

**Face your fears:** Another way to strengthen your will is to face your fears. Most fears that we have are toward things that are not harmful. There are rational fears and irrational fears. Rational fears are immediate dangers to avoid. On the other hand we need to face irrational fears. If you are afraid of rejection, face the challenge, rejection is not an immediate danger, it is just a response we interpret as personal that hurts our feelings.

For a week do something daily to face your irrational fears. First make a list, such as are you afraid to talk to someone? Are you afraid to ask your boss for a raise that you feel that you deserve? Are you afraid of spiders? Write down those fears.

_____

_____

_____

_____

_____

_____

_____

_____

_____

_____

_____

_____

_____

If it is spiders, make sure that it isn't poisonous. Other than the black widow there are no poisonous spiders in the east coast of the United States. In other areas they have a few poisonous spiders such as the brown recluse.

If you see a spider in the house, for example overcome your fear and cup it in your hand and take it outside. If you are afraid of losing someone who isn't healthy in your life at all, face the fear and depart from that person. You will feel better in the long run. Face those fears.

**Delay Gratification:** What I mean by this is that we sometime give into pleasures that are bad for us in the long run. Some alcoholics put off drinking until a certain time. Doing this may actually help them kick the habit. Many times we procrastinate when we know there are things that we need to do. Instead we are compulsively indulging in something that gives us instant pleasure; meanwhile what needs to be done never gets done. Therefore exercise that willpower to put off that instant gratification and do what needs to be done before you get back to your pleasure.

**Replacing habits:** This exercise of willpower is too substitute bad habits with good habits. We are creatures of habit and therefore we are not designed to do nothing. We cannot just quit a bad habit and do nothing. We have to say yes to something that will benefit us. Many times our bad habits get in the way of our goals. Make a list of the things you do during the day. Examine each habit and mark down the ones that are interfering with your goals, in another column, write down what you can substitute that will cause you to be closer to your goals. Here is example.

| List of habits | Bad Habits | Replace with Good habits |
|---|---|---|
| Get up to get ready for work at last minute. Come home from stressful day. Eat and drink a beer to relax. Stay up late and continue the cycle again. | Last minute rushing. Drinking a beer to relax. Staying up late. | Get up earlier and take time. Perhaps meditate and relax upon awakening. The day probably wouldn't be stressful if I didn't start my day rushing not to be late. Instead of drinking a beer, exercise to relax. Go to bed at a reasonable time every night at the same time. |

**Replace emotions:** When you feel an emotion that is unhealthy, such as depression or rage, do not fight it. Do not get lost in dark thoughts. Just feel. Getting lost in dark thoughts or going berserk actually stop you from experiencing the emotions fully while the dark thoughts continue to feed it. The idea is to become aware and replace the feeling. Don't try to change it, just replace it. Nurse the thoughts that will generate the feelings that you want. Imagine the opposite of what it is that is making you feel depress for example.

1. When did you notice you were depressed?

_____

_____

_____

_____

2. What caused your depression?

_____

_____

_____

_____

3. Do you feel that you failed a goal? If so write down detail.

_____

_____

_____

_____

4. Did an experience that is personal make you feel certain aspects of yourself? Describe those feelings and why do you believe this to be true about yourself.

_____

_____

_____

_____

If you are feeling depressed right now, this may not be easy to do. For when we are depressed, we feel hopeless and feel as if nothing is going to work. We think that we are so special that something is wrong with us. We tend to feel that it may work for others, but not for us.

5. Opposite scenario. Write down and imagine that the experience is what you would like to happen that is different than what actually did. Example, see yourself happily paying your bills, because you know that you have enough money. Or see that the girl you want to pursue is in a happy relationship with you. This may be hard at first, because it may be overwhelming and our current situation is reality to us, while what we want, isn't at the moment. With practice you are changing your reality.

_____

_____

_____

_____

# Desire

Desire is the food for the will. Many believe that lack of desire is caused by depression. Actually, it's the other way around. Lack of desire is the root of depression. Sometimes our diet is poor. That poor diet may cause a chemical imbalance to where we feel fatigue. The fatigue then leads to lack of desire and procrastination. In due time, because we are procrastinating we are hurting ourselves because our needs are not getting met. That hurt becomes anger, and anger in a passive way turns inward and leads to depression. This is an example of a chemical imbalance leading to lack of desire and that leading to depression. Not handling stress can also cause depression. As I said in the first chapter, that stress creates a fight or flight response. If one reacts in a passive or passive aggressive or aggressive approach to the situation one's needs are not getting met. Passiveness or passive aggression also leads to procrastination. Procrastination is just a mild form of anxiety. Anxiety kills desire which usually follows with depression.

**Stop Musturbating:** In the last chapter I mention it's ok to masturbate. In this chapter I am suggesting one to not musturbate. There is a difference. Musturbation is being caught up in the thoughts of, 'must, should, have to and shouldn't have. When we are caught up in these thoughts we become a slave to our emotions. We identify ourselves with them. These words lead to anxiety which hinder us from solving our problems. It weakens the desire that is needed to solve and achieve goals. Not only do these irrational thoughts hinder desire they block one from the ability to even solve the problem. Anxiety causes one to freeze, and that is what procrastination is. This is usually why anxiety comes before depression. Yeshua the great teacher also known as Jesus and Sananda said, "Cease looking for proof outside yourself, and believe in Yourselves, You are gods." Therefore do not be too attach to things, they are transient. The core of the true Buddhist teaching is that 'all is transitory.' Nothing is permanent therefore no needed to become too attach to anything that is fleeting. In Anonymous groups there is a saying, 'This too shall pass" it is the same thing. Situations, people, even our feelings are transient. When we are hurt it is only temporally. Too many people have committed suicide because they got caught up in the erroneous belief that the pain they are feeling will never go away.

Suicide is just a permanent solution to a temporally problem. When we have thoughts such as "I *must* have a relationship with

Amy, if I don't then it's the end of my world," This type of thinking is illogical and causes misery. Too many times we get caught up in this musturbatory thinking. Another example is "This *should*n't have happened; now everything is messed up." These thoughts are illogical because they are not true. Is your world really ended if you do not have a relationship with Amy? I don't think so. It may hurt, but your world still goes on. Because you made a mistake, does that mean everything is fucked up? Most likely everything is not going to be ruined because you made a mistake. To overcome these irrational thoughts is called Rational Emotive Behavior Therapy, which is a major part in psychology today. It is the disputing of irrational beliefs.

Science is flexible, non-dogmatic and full of facts and logical thinking. Even though logical thinking does not contradict itself, it holds two opposite views at the same time. It avoids rigid all or nothing thinking and sees reality as two sided characteristics. Example would be one is not totally good or totally bad, we have both characteristics. That also means that there is no being that is totally good or totally evil. We all have both even if one aspect dominates more than the other. Therefore we need to stop judging world events in an all or nothing absolute way. Science assumes events usually follow the law of certainty.

When Sananda said, "Judge not, that you be judged, for with what judgment you judge, you shall not be judge: and what measure you mete, it shall be measured to you again." What this refers to is not to make a final decision about circumstances, to do so means you made a final decision about the course of your life. If your decision about life is that it sucks, then that is how the world will be reflected back to you. Many believe that "seeing is believing," when it actually is "believing is seeing." We see what we expect to see and what we see might not always be actuality. Sananada is a great scientist and when he taught through his parables, he was teaching science.

Science is skeptical of all ideas in the absolute; it accepts new theories as new information comes through. It doesn't support any ideas that can be falsified such as a invisible devil in the world that causes all the evils in the world. It doesn't say that the supernatural doesn't exist, since there is no way to prove they do or do not, it isn't included in the sphere of science.

Science doesn't support the idea of deserving and undeserving, that good acts are rewarded and that bad acts are punished.

When you are upset about something where you are depressed, self-pitying, anxious, or doing something against you own best interest, assumed that you are thinking unscientifically.

Examples. "Since I strongly love you, you have to love me." This is unrealistic and against the facts of life. "Since I hurt others I'm doom to burn in hell forever," "Since I'm a good person, then things will work out," These two cannot be proven.

Think back to your childhood when something you say terrible happened. Maybe your father beat you in front of all your friends at the Wave Pool and you were embarrassed, especially one of the witnesses was a girl you liked. Remember what you told yourself to make this event so traumatic. Were you telling yourself for example? "My father shouldn't have beaten me in front of everyone, especially at the Wave pool,' did this event really has an effect on the course of your life? Most likely it did not. Write down an event you thought was terrible.

*I decide I'm going to ask Amy out.*

*and i'm nervous*

Now that you wrote down the incident, write down in first column what were your beliefs. Then dispute them and write rational beliefs.

| Beliefs | Dispute | Rational Beliefs |
|---------|---------|------------------|
| 1.She must not reject me or that means I'm worthless. | 1.Why does it mean that? | 1. I would like for Amy to say yes, if she doesn't, it doesn't make me less worthy. |
| 2.If she says no, it will be too painful; I won't be able to bear it. | 2.Why would the pain be too unbearable? | 2. I am not what I experience. Emotional pain will pass and is not putting anyone in immediate danger. |
| 3. I must ease the pain with drugs or alcohol or I won't function. | 3. Do I need drugs? | |
| 4. Something must be wrong with me, and I'm unlovable person if I get rejected. | 4. Does that mean I'm unlovable and something wrong with me? | 3. Nope, I just want it. 4. That is just her opinion, and I'm ok as I am. |
| 5. I must be loved by someone I really care about. | 5. Does that person have to love me, because I love them? | 5. It would be nice if they did, but that just isn't how life is. Sometimes they do, sometimes they don't. |

Therefore the idea is to come to the realization that it is about having the take it or leave it attitude. When it matters too much where we say it must, or should, causes unnecessary stress.

To know more about Rational Emotive Therapy check out "How to stubbornly Refuse to Make Yourself Miserable About Anything Yes Everything" by Albert Ellis, Ph.D.

**Are you the dream or the dreamer:** Most of us get caught up in believing that we are the dream. In sleep we don't know that we are dreaming and sometimes become victims of our own creations. Everything that we experience in our sleeping dream is a manifestation of your mind. This is an example of our sleeping dream, but in this world we live in is also a dream. If you seen the movie 'the matrix' you would understand what I mean. In the movie everyone is lying in tubes while interacting with each other in a holographic world that they perceive as reality. In this world everything is holographic. Space is just an illusion and is actually filled with the same energy that everything that you see is made from. Electromagnetic fields that radiate from fractals that we call objects give us the appearance of things being solid. When two magnets have same poles they repel each other, it's the same with objects that appear solid. The electromagnetic field frequency also sends impulses to our brain where we feel touch as we interpret as textures from these fractals.

The Buddhist calls this hologram, Mara the Tempter, the Lord of the Abyss of Hallucinations. This illusion is necessary for growth, and at the same time we can get lost if we are not careful. Anything that you can experience isn't you. If you can experience emotions that mean that you are not your emotions. This book that you are reading, you are experiencing it, therefore it is not you. The Buddhist has a saying, "If you meet the Buddha on the road, kill him." What this means is that the Buddha is your true self that is the experiencer that is the glue of the universe. If you identify with an experience, then it isn't you, therefore kill the identification with it. Most of us identify with our emotions, our job title, our relationships. Because of this identifying with these things we falsely believe is us, we are afraid to lose our job title, afraid to lose our relationships because to do so means to us, we lose ourselves. We believe that we will become lost and cease to exist. It is these irrational beliefs that cause us to fear change it causes us not to change, because we think if we change our emotional beliefs, and then we lose our identity. Having these beliefs is believing that you are the dream. This is no different than believing that you are the character on the stage that is stuck in the role that was written for them.

Realizing that you are the dreamer is realizing those traits are not you, they are what you experience. You also know and accept that all things are transitory. Whatever you experience, good or bad shall pass. All is transitory. Since you are not your emotions, then you can chose to change them.

If a situation causes you emotional pain, you know it's not you and shall pass. This can help overcoming rejection, because any emotional pain that you experience from rejection will pass. The hurt is not an immediate danger to your well being, it is just an unpleasant experience.

Our true Self is the God within. The same God within me is also the same God within you and everyone else. Separation is an illusion. A tub full of sponges immersed in water, the water is in every sponge, but there is only one water. Just like water, there is only one Self, one Experiencer, and one Dreamer. The only thing that makes each of us individuals is our memories due to what we experienced.

This dream, what we call reality has the same characteristics as our sleeping dream, even though it may be a little more firm. In our sleeping dream, the more lucid we become the more control that we have over the dream. In this world we call reality, the more lucid that we become in our daily lives, the more mastery that you will have. In our sleeping dream all the characters we create are a reflection of our desires and fears. In waking life, all the people we meet are also a reflection of our desires and fears. Just like the sleeping dream, we just didn't create them; we just subconsciously invited them into our life. In the dream we realize what we experience shall pass. If we experience pain, we know that it is just a dream, and that we can chose something else.

Navy Seals for example don't identify with the pain they go through in training. They have to swim 500 yards at the minimum of 12:30 seconds. Within two minutes they have to do 42 to 100 pushups. They don't let pain slow them down. The key is their desire. Their desire to be on the military elite fighting team is stronger than their avoidance to any pain that may get in the way. Therefore the key to not to identify with the pain is desire.

**Strengthen your Desires:** Desire is the force that manifests all things. It is what feeds the will. Desire is love and without it, there is no will. Desire is the motivating force for all Creation. Whatever man desires, the God within will create. Law of Gravity is the Law of Desire. From the center of the black hole comes desire. As I said before from that comes electricity. We live in an electric universe. All things have an electric awareness of itself to some degree. Like keys on a piano where each sound is slightly different than the key before, each manifestation is more aware than the previous awareness before it. Electricity keeps fracturing itself to where we get an atom that has one proton which is hydrogen. Hydrogen atoms are fractals of the whole. Every aspect of the atom has all the information as the original source. Just like letters in the alphabet when arranged together in a certain way makes words, when electricity fractals in a certain pattern you get the makeup of all parts of the atom. The hydrogen atom electric awareness is limited. When the next set of atoms comes into play such as the helium atom that has two protons, this set of atoms has more electric awareness than the previous hydrogen atoms and its awareness is still limited. This electric awareness continues in each set of atoms that are manifested.

When carbon which has 6 protons is mixed with other minerals and water, two major chemical compounds is formed. That chemical is called Ribonucleic acid (RNA) and deoxyribonucleic acid (DNA). DNA is stored as a code made up of four chemical bases which is adenine (A), guanine (G), cytosine (C), and thymine (T). Each base that pairs together is attached to a sugar molecule and phosphate molecule which forms a nucleotide that forms strands. It is how these are arranged that determines the information for building and maintaining an organism that is being formed. This all starts from the sea and plant cell such as

66

bacteria is the first that comes from this. The electric awareness still evolves. Plants are more aware than minerals. Sea plants evolve in the sea. Eventually the animal cell is produce and you get the ameba and fish, these animals have more electric awareness than the plants, soon you get crustaceans and insects that can walk on land. Then comes amphibians and reptiles then birds and land mammals. Each manifestation has more electric awareness than the previous, but still limited. When it comes to humans who DNA consist of about 3 billion bases and more than 99% of those bases are the same in all people. When it comes to humans the electric awareness is the most evolve, and when it comes to us, there is no limitation. We have the ability to exercise the will to become ever more electrically aware. No matter how much we become aware, there is more, for the information that we have that links all things that is of the whole is unlimited and within us as in all things.

Due to our unlimited level of awareness potential, we can manifest anything that we desire, no matter what it is. The stronger the desire, the more powerful the manifestation. We are co-creators for any desire of man is, therefore, a two-way extension of the Light of that idea from the Source. Man must co-create in according to the Laws of Creation.

Desire leads to action, we wouldn't move at all if we didn't desire something. Depression comes forth from when we lack desire. Conventional doctors say lack of desire is the effect of depression, they say if we cure the depression, then the desire for things we lost interest in will come back. On the contrary we can overcome depression by bringing desire back into our lives. If we are depressed and believe that we need to overcome our depression in order to get back our desire, we might spend years looking for the source of our depression.

As co-creators, creating can be healing to the mind, especially for PTSD and Bipolar. It helps the mind calm down and concentrate on projects.

Creating can help build confidence and self esteem. Desire is what is needed to express ourselves as co-creators. Many mistakenly think to be on a spiritual path, desire is what hinders us from the path. This is not so, desire is essential to our existence, without desire nothing would exist. When we are hungry, we have the desire to eat. We fulfill that desire and we are satisfied until hunger arises in us again. Everything is transitory. Desires lead us to go find a partner so that we procreate life. Even desires that distract us are necessary for growth. There are four levels of desires.

1. No desire.
2. Trying, but not giving our all.
3. Making an effort and keeping focus on our goal.
4. Making it happen, no matter what.

The thing is that most people function on level 2 which is just trying, and barely making it to level 3. When one is depressed, they are usually on level one, which is no desire. Without desire we feel lost in the dark. In darkness we must illuminate so that we can see. The Light is every positive emotion we can imagine that flows from the All That Is. That positive emotion is love which is desire.

Sharing is a way to co-create and bring feelings of being part of something. Do something to be part of the community or to help others. Every time we share we become proactive. When we are proactive, we then are not being reactive. Proactively leads to being co-creators like the Light of Creator. When we are, we are infinity with the Light.

**Pausing:** Pausing can be beneficial, and we must learn to pause before we react. In any situation, whether it brings pleasure or pain, we are tempted to react without thinking. When we are reactive, we disconnect from the Light. The idea is to be vigilant and choose to be conscious instead of running on autopilot. Relying on old patterns will not lead us into the Light, but pausing between stimulus and your response will.

**Knowing what you want:** Many of us do not even really know what we want. To want something, you must with all your heart want it. How can you desire something that you are not even sure what it is you want.

Ask yourself these questions. Do you want money? Or is it the security that you want from it? Do you want sex? Or do you want a romantic relationship with someone we love that loves us back? When we ask these questions, it turns out what we want is the lasting feelings that is associated with it. By pausing we consider our responses carefully instead of reacting to choices that will leave us empty in a short while. Write down what it is you want. Then in next column write what feelings they bring you and what you want from it.

| What you want | Feelings it will bring |
|---|---|
| I want a romantic relationship with Josephine. | Being with her will add to me feeling as if I'm the luckiest man in the world. I would feel as if I can accomplish anything in the universe. |
| I want to get all my books out there to the public. | To do this will help me feel as if I am helping a lot of people. |
| I want a million dollars | For security and to be able to help people in many areas, philanthropy in institutions that supports my goal into helping to bring world peace. And as source to get my books really out there through advertizing and book signings and lectures. |
| I want to lose weight | This means more energy to achieve everything else I listed prior. Have better health and feel better. That means more money, better chance to get books out more and better chance for romantic relationship. |

When you know what you want, imagine that you have it, feel the feelings of having what you want. Use all your senses in seeing that you have it. Smell the perfume, feel the textures, etc. See what you want you already have it. See yourself already in the situation. Desire it with all your heart. Feel yourself in a romantic relationship, feel yourself thin, etc.

This will strengthen your personal power. When one's personal power is weak one tends to give away their power as a way to avoid conflict.

**Temporally pain vs. suffering:** When it come to conflict, many of us want to keep the peace. We must not give our personal power to others. It is best to be proactive and feel temporally discomfort by speaking the truth than to suffer lifelong misery. Too many times we keep our mouth shut and let others run over on us, because we want to avoid conflict. Stand up and face the challenge. That awkward situation is there so that you can face it to learn and grow. Avoiding conflict slows down your growth process. When you just cope with the pain of not standing up to what needs to be said, your pain builds up. You become bitter and you are never happy while thinking the world is out to get you while you're trying to be Mr. Nice Guy/Girl. Part of growth is dealing with people on a daily basis. Allowing this unnecessary pain to build up means your needs are not getting met, and this stress can cause stomach acids to over produce leading to acid reflex or stomach ulcers. Therefore be assertive and tell others the truth about your needs and wants, not only will you most likely get your needs met, you will grow from facing the challenge of expressing yourself assertively. This is how you achieve personal power.

# THE FOURTH SPIRAL
## (Element *Air*)

The Fourth spiral of the Power Center is located in the heart area. It is the heart energy center. It is associated with the element Air. This Power Center is about Love. Here is a correspondent of the symbolism of this power center.

**Element:** Air
**Function:** Love, compassion
**Glands:** Thymus
**Unbalances:** Asthma, heart disease, lung disease
**Color:** green
**Sephira:** Tiphareth

This Power Center is associated with Love. Each of the vortexes is associated with love. They are all connected. It is most unlikely you will have 1 very strong vortex while very weak in others, though it is possible. One affects the others. Just like keys on the piano or colors of a rainbow, each frequency is slightly different than the previous. In the first power Center is survival, one has to have self love to even be able to stand on their own two feet. When we don't love ourselves, then we feel that we need a crutch. In the second Power Center for us to be open to intimacy we first develop our bonding with our mother. This bonding determines how much self esteem and self worth we have, which again is first have to do with loving ourselves. The third power Center is associated with personal power. One has to be able to respect themselves enough to not give their power away to others, our emotions and impulsiveness. Now we come into the fourth Power Center.

The fourth spiral is the neutral connector of the soul. It connects the three male vortexes at the bottom with the three female vortexes at the top. It controls the circulatory system of the soul.

When the heart is unbalanced, we get stuck in the lower vortexes. One lacks personal power, intimacy problems and standing on their own two feet. In the Egyptian book of "Coming Forth By Day" the heart is weighed on the scales against the feather of truth. (Figure 4.1) If it is too heavy it is fed to the crocodile Ammut. The image of the power centers is the crocodile sitting with its closed mouth between the three centers and the fourth center of the heart. It is symbolic that if you cannot rise beyond the three bottom centers, then the crocodile is there to devour your heart. This devouring is reincarnation with no memories of your formal life.

If your heart is light then you pass into the door of immortality, which means you continue to consciously retain your memories by having a radiant body.

When our heart center is weak we identify with our body, our relationships and our experiences. Air is the element for this energy center, air represents freedom. When we fall in love we feel like we are walking on air. When we grasp too tightly to our love, we suffocate our beloved, which is no different than depriving them of air.

This suffocation is due to fear of loss; this individual identifies themselves with their relationship. They feel if they lost their relationship they will lose their identity. One tends to sabotage their relationships with distrust, anger or fear that they will lose their independence if they rely too much on others. With this energy center being weak, one tends to always be on guard and tend to please others because they feel it is the only way someone can love them.

This attachment to their experiences is what causes the loss of memories in the previous life when reincarnation takes place. Let me explain, when one loses what they identify with, they feel lost. Example, Joe believes that he is his job title and relationships. Joe loses his job and romantic partner. He feels so lost that he doesn't know how to cope. He heads to the bar and burry his sorrows into alcohol. The alcohol is how he copes, it makes him temporally forget.

Figure 4.1

The emotional state that you have while living, you take with you. Being dead doesn't make one smarter or wiser. Therefore if one identifies with their body and other experiences when they are alive, they will still identify with those same things after death.

The average person who is attached to their body and experiences will feel this lost when everything that they identified with is ripped away from them. They lost their body, their job title, and their relationships with all they knew. They now need a way to cope with this lost. The light at the end of the tunnel is like a drug that the dead emerge themselves into. Within the light brings feelings of bliss that the dead enter to cope with the lost of their previous life. In this blissful light in time one forgets all about their previous life. In the movie Casper for example, he has been a ghost so long that he doesn't even remember his formal life. He doesn't remember who he is, or his family. Those who enter into the light disintegrate as they reincarnate without any conscious memories of their previous lives. On the other had when your heart energy center is strong, you realize that you are not your body. You come to realize that you are none of your experiences and the true you is the God within. This awareness comes through meditation. This will cause you to develop a radiant body to where you do not have to enter the light; instead you produce your own light. Since there is no need to cope by entering into the light, you will consciously retain all your memories. This is true immortality.

The heart is the link between the higher and lower energy centers. All the energy centers have a pair except the heart. The pairs are linked through a spiral connection. The heart is at the end of the point of the spiral (figure 4.2).

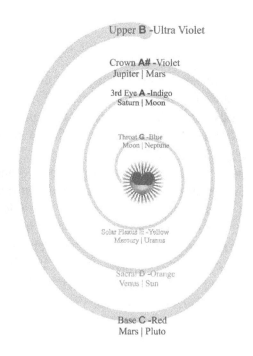

Figure 4.2
Spiral point ending at the heart

The root center's mate and counterpart is the crown. The sex center and third eye center are counterparts. The personal power counterpart is the throat center as you realize a main part of exercising personal power is through the voice. In the center of our being is the full integration into the heart.

As I said air symbolizes freedom and when your heart center is strong it is possible for astral flight. Breath also takes a role in the heart center.

If you want to influence the body through the mind, you would through controlling the breath. Mastering the breath can calm the mind. Opening this heart center takes an understanding of the control of the breath. In practices of ancient Chinese art of energy exercise called Chi Kung, this control of breath and energy was to produce strength, rejuvenation and longevity. The ancient Taoist believed that it can impart immortality.

Chi Kung combines secret ancient breathing techniques with postures and movements to cultivate 'Chi" (energy that sustains all life). Long term Chi Kung practices improve every human physiological function, such as circulation, respiration, skeleton strength, metabolism, immune system and the neuro-muscular function. For more than 5000 years Chinese have used this for prevention and treatment of disease, strengthening the body, improving intelligence, spiritual development, extending longevity and developing hidden powers.

This also improves the astral circulation as well, which is the heart center and helps pure the heart

*"Purification of the heart (consciousness) leads to the* **HIGHEST GOOD: ETERNAL LIFE** *and Supreme Peace."* *-Egyptian proverb.*

Purification of the heart isn't being without sin as many believe. It is about having that laser beam focus about what your goal is in life. When your heart is tainted, there is ambivalence in your heart, that ambivalence is caused by a weak desire which usually due to addiction to our current comfort zone. When we are stuck in our current comfort zone, we are afraid to move into unknown territories. This fear weakens our will, hindering us to move forward. As in the comic book story of Green Lantern, will is the opposite of fear. In the comics, will is the color of green and this is the color of the heart center. Will is more associated in the personal power center, but it is the start to developing a pure heart. As I said in last chapter strengthening your desires is how you strengthen the will. Strengthening your will is the key to a pure heart. In the Egyptian book 'Coming Forth By Day' the heart must be pure to not be too heavy when weighed against the feather of truth from Maat. Maat means justice and also means the way; the way is that of following the Laws of Creation, in Chinese its Tao. The Laws of Creation is the Laws of Nature. The word nature is Greek word that originates from the Egyptian word Neter which means God or Divine. Therefore there is no separation of nature or the Divine. Therefore God is not supernatural, all is natural, and to try to separate ourselves from nature just degrades us. We are self aware animals and the only thing that makes us different than other animals is our potential of unlimited self awareness. Our goal is to find this hidden divinity within. This hidden divinity is within all, and since we are a manifestation of it, to find it is to seek within. That is by meditation and self reflection.

The symbol of the heart energy center is the two interlacing triangles which is the six pointed star. This as I mention in the introduction is the symbol of All That Is. Some sources say the Pleiadians use it as a symbol for brotherhood. This is also the symbol of the Sacred Marriage and the Sacred Heart of Jesus. This is the star of radiance that comes from an open heart. (Figure 4.3). This is the only power center that is neutral and doesn't have a partner. All the other power centers are paired except the heart center where the two triangles intercept. In the element table, all the elements have a pair except the element carbon that is perfectly balanced and also the element that is the bases of organic life.

Figure 4.3
The Sacred Heart

**Opening your heart:** Love is about loving unconditionally, that is love doesn't have expectations nor obligations. Love doesn't have conditions where it says, "I will do this for you, if you do this for me," or "I'll love you if you let me mold you into the image that I want you to be." Love is about accepting people and things as they are. Too many of us have our guard up because we are afraid that our egos will get hurt. We are so protective of our egos, that we are afraid that by opening our heart we will be vulnerable to being hurt. We are afraid that individual may have ulterior motives and afraid to give them a chance. No one has ever died from a hurt ego. As I said before, "this too shall pass."

For a week at least try to see the good in everyone that you encounter, it may not be easy at first. Give others a benefit of a doubt unless they give you reason not to. By seeing the good in others, will help you see the good in you. Many of us have trouble seeing the good in ourselves, so we assume others won't see what we believe is not there, and settle for unhealthy relationships because we figure who would want us, so we settle for the abuser because we find it hard to believe that someone worthy will even like us.

Also be kind and generous. Sometimes we may encounter someone with a nasty attitude and our first response is to take it personally and go to their level by snapping back. They may just have this nasty attitude because they had a bad day and has nothing to do with you. Write down your experiences of how this may turn out by not stepping to their level.

For example the cable guy shows up at your door with a nasty attitude. Instead of stooping to his level, have him open up to you about his day. He may surprise you by venting to you about what a bad day he had and feel better because you were kind enough to listen. By the time he fixes your service and leave, he is now leaving in better spirits. Not only does he feel better, you also feel better that you was able to make someone feel better.

_____

_____

_____

_____

_____

Another exercise that you can do is doing something good for someone without expecting anything back in return. Let go of the concern that you are setting yourself up to be taken advantage of. Many think love is weak, when actually love is what brings peace of mind.

Sananda said, "Love thy neighbor," he understood the science behind this. Sananda known as Jesus was more than just a philosopher and teacher. He was a politician and also a scientist. He took on the role as a Priest and King after John the Baptist's death who was possibly a priest of the Temple of Isis. The immersion of water as an initiation is a ritual that originated in Egypt.

When you love your neighbor you are aligning yourself in harmony with the greatest power in the universe. You become in synch with the Laws of Creation which is ruled by the force of love.

According to Meir and other sources, before 226,000 B.C. the Lyrians from the constellation of Lyra was warriors who were space Vikings that went out and conquered anything that they can. They migrated to Orion, Hyades and the Pleiades. Perhaps some of this is reflected in Norse Mythology, as well as Sumerian. When a wise leader (Yshwish) named Pleja came to rule, things changed as she had colonized Earth, Mars and Milona. Milona supposedly was a planet that existed beyond the orbit of Mars. Milona was destroyed as Mars was thrown out of orbit destroying all life upon it.

Pleja brought peace and that is by having an open heart. Having an open heart is how we survive. We survive by working together.

*"Tie two birds together even though you have four wings you cannot fly,"*

–The Blind Man, (The Silent Flute)

*"But if you fly side by side, you can fly farther than you ever could alone,"*

–Tatiana.

This means that if you are too attached to someone due to fear of loss, you cannot move anywhere; instead you will just destroy the one you are attached to. I don't necessary mean destroy them on a fatal attraction scenario. Your smothering by not allowing them to breathe will cause their destruction. On the other hand by working together as a team allowing everyone to do their own thing, then you can all soar to the heights of heaven.

Here is a parable by an unknown author.

The Swami was having a conversation with Lord Shiva one day and said Lord, "I would like to know what heaven and hell are like".

Lord Shiva led the Swami to two doors.

He opened one of the doors and the Swami looked in. In the middle of the room was a large round table. In the middle of the table was a large pot of stew, which smelled delicious and made the Swami's mouth water.

The people sitting around the table were thin and sickly. They appeared to be famished. They were holding spoons with very long handles that were strapped to their arms and each found it possible to reach into the pot of stew and take a spoonful.

However, the handle was longer than their arms; they could not get the spoons back into their mouths.

The Swami shuddered at the sight of their misery and suffering. Lord Shiva said, "You have seen hell".

They went to the next room and opened the door. It was exactly the same as the first one. There was the large round table with the large pot of stew which made the holy man's mouth water. The people were equipped with the same long-handled spoons, but here the people were well nourished and plump, laughing and talking.

The Swami said, "I don't understand".

"It is simple", said Lord Shiva, "It requires but one skill. You see they have learned to feed each other, while the greedy think only of themselves".

This parable shows how self centeredness doesn't get anyone anywhere. When we are too concerned about getting our ego hurt we are being self centered. When we have the attitude, I won't do for you, unless you do for me, that is self-centeredness.

Before Pleja came to be the Queen of Wisdom the Lyrians caused the destruction of thousands of worlds. Those who honor the peace loving ways of Pleja call themselves Plejarans. The Pleiades star system was also named after her. Love is what causes good things to happen to you, lack of love causes bad things to happen to you. Many times we don't even realize that we are lacking love. We feel ok, and so caught up in ourselves that we don't even realizing what's going on outside ourselves. When we complain about circumstances we are not exercising love, and the complaining brings more of what you are complaining about. Even doing volunteer work for the Salvation Army or Children's Hospital is good therapy and will open your heart. This is also a good exercise for getting rid of depression. It gives one the feeling that they have a place and worthy place in the world. The idea is instead of waiting for a miracle is to be a miracle daily in someone else's life.

Love is action. Many think it is just a feeling. The feelings of love are the side effect from love. Love is a verb and the feeling is the fruit of love. Reactive individuals make love a feeling. They are just driven by their feelings. If they don't feel love, they refuse to act.

Proactive individuals for example make love a verb. It is something that you do, the sacrifices that you make, the giving of the self. Love is action, and to love others is to show actions that serve, appreciate, listen, empathize and make sacrifices. Take a break and make time to show love. Maybe you haven't called someone that you need to call. Maybe you are putting off writing that letter that is needed to a dear friend who lives some distance. Make that sacrifice and make some time for others. You can even make an appointment to spend time or make that phone call to say, "Hello."

Here is another exercise to at least give it a try for a week. Talk only about the stuff you love. Even if some things that happen during the day that you didn't like, bypass that and be grateful for the things you did like that day and talk only about that. You can also write down all the things you love and are grateful for each day during this exercise.

_____

_____

_____

_____

_____

_____

People, who have good lives, talk more about what they love than what they do not.

**Power of Feeling:** *"Feel, it is like a finger pointing to the moon, don't concentrate on the finger or you will miss all the heavenly glory,"*
– Bruce Lee.

Just by focusing on thinking positive isn't enough, you must feel what you want. Thinking positive is the finger pointing the way. It all begins with thought, but you must generate feeling.

81

Thoughts have no power without feeling. The energy centers express the feelings that you have, and these feelings send out waves to attract those people and circumstances that are on the same vibration as your feelings. All good feelings come from love and the more you give love, are the more love you receive. Gratitude and satisfaction are emotions that feel good. Gratitude is the opposite of complaining.

Too many times we feel good about something for ten minutes, and then suddenly our mood is thrown off when something we experience is uncomfortable. We spend 10 minutes with good feeling, but spend an hour with bad feeling, and throughout the day, we wind up spending hours with bad feelings and the rest of the time other than for ten minutes, we just feel okay.

Feeling just okay isn't feelings of good; they are just okay feelings which just manifest okay mediocre life. If you don't feel good about your relationships, then your relationships will not improve. If you don't feel good about money, such as feeling dread every time you pay bills, then your financial situation will not improve. When you change the way you feel, then you will change your life. You must feel good about paying your bills for your financial situation to improve. If you want your relationship to improve, you must have good feelings toward it first. To generate good feeling when it comes to paying bills, see yourself as donating charity to the company for their good services. In relationships, have gratitude towards what it is that makes you feel good. Feel good about what you want and feel as if it has taken place. Imagine the joy of having it.

To generate the feelings, one must take action. It is more than just imagination. This triggers the feelings, but you must also take action toward those goals. Exert willpower to take the actions that is needed to feel your goals. Imagination, knowing that it will come, exerts actions of service that leads you closer to your goals.

**Healing:** Love has the power to heal. Heal means to make whole. When we are in the process of healing, we are reclaiming lost parts of ourselves. When we are imbalanced we are not whole. To become whole is a process of recovery. To be in harmony with the Laws of Creation one must constantly be in recovery. Since we have the potentials to have unlimited self awareness, we must take action daily to become more aware than the day before. We should work on being better than we was yesterday. When we become complacent and don't exercise our will to become better we feel discomfort. That discomfort comes in the form of feeling bad. When we feel bad we are out of balance and those bad feelings causes' unpleasant circumstances.

Disease is when you are not in the natural state of "ease." This means your natural state of ease is imbalanced or disrupted either physically or mentally or both. The discomfort from being not at ease is a necessity. The discomfort is a signal that tells you that you are out of balance. The discomfort comes as mental agitation or physical discomfort. This means you must be balanced to get better. When you feel good, you heal faster because there is no discomfort.

Love is the force that heals. When we are lacking love we are out of balance with the Laws of Creation. Bad feelings are the discomfort that if not dealt with causes a domino effect of chaos. If you feel bad it will reflect in your behavior. All the irrational choices made due to insecurity, greed, laziness, anger, etc. are all due to discomfort that causes us to feel bad.

When you show compassion, bonding and understanding, you have the urge to heal. When we play we feel good. During the time of playing we are so caught up in the moment that we have no worries. Dolphins and humans have so many similar traits. Humans and dolphins are almost the only animals that play until adulthood. They are Sea mammals that have arguably said to be the closest spiritually, intellectual and social link to humans of all the sea creatures. Recently the history channel presented a document called "Mermaid the Body Found' and Mermaid New Evidence" if this information is correct, then dolphins may not be the only ones. From the source of the examination of the body of the mermaid, mermaids are mammals like dolphins.

Perhaps there is some common ancestry to mermaids if they do exist. Since the beginning in ancient text, descriptions of mermaids have been described.

According to ancient Sumerian text the Sumerians told about a watery planet named Tiamat. This was supposedly 4.5 billions of years ago. This watery planet was twice the size of earth. According to the Sumerians, one of the moons from the planet Niburu struck Tiamat and split it in two. In time both halves became Earth and Milona. According to the text 3500 years later when the moon came around again it hit the second half and smashed it into smithereens. According to Meir planet Milona planet was destroyed by war. In both views the debris that was left became the asteroid belt.

Is it possible that on Tiamat the little bit of land was ruled by dinosaurs while in the water the planet was ruled by species such as Mermaids.

Legend speaks about the God Ea who was known as God of Water and was honored by the zodiacal signs of *Aquarius* and *Pisces*, and the "priests who oversaw his worship" were dressed as *Fishmen*. Later the Greeks described the Oannes who spoke as a human that had the appearance of a fish that came from the sea to teach mankind and returned to the sea at night.

Later a disciple of Aristotle wrote about a second visitation of more beings like that of Oannes that came from the sea to teach mankind. In the Sumerian text it is mentioned that Ea created the race of modern humans. Perhaps can it be that our ancestors came from a humanoid species from the sea, and that some survivals of Tiamat are still here on this planet which was once Tiamat? If this is so, this could be the explanation why we have aquatic features such as webbed fingers, almost hairless bodies, as hair in water slows down movement. Human babies automatically hold their breaths and automatically know how to swim, but we are the only land animal that has to be taught how to walk. It is as though through genetic memory swimming is natural from our ancestors, whereas walking is not.

The Dogon tribe in Africa mentioned fish people taught them about the orbital mechanics of Sirius and that their ancestors are people from the Sirius star system. The Dogon are famous for their astronomical knowledge taught to them thousands of years ago. Mermaids if they exist may also have come from Sirius. Shipwrecked passengers who seen them thought of them as demons while the mermaids was trying to assist them with healing. Christopher Columbus also claims he saw a mermaid and also a UFO during his voyage.

Johnny Sands a contactee who have been interrogated by the Men in Black have seen extraterrestrial beings (Figure 4.4) that had wide flat nose and gills. The Men in Black told him that there is a planet that is half water and half land that resided in Sirius star system.

Figure 4.4
Aquatic Extraterrestrial

What the dolphins and mermaids can teach us if mermaids exist is that they can teach us how to play. To teach us not to take life too seriously and to use delight as a motivation. Fun, play, enthusiasm radiates from most dolphins. Dolphins love to swim, play, make love and eat herring. They fish in group cooperation and each gets fed. They live in many attracting qualities: delight, joy, fun, and play.

Why so serious son? Ask the Joker. Playing strengthens social bonds and creates an inventive brain and restful mind. Dolphins think in wholeness. The glass isn't half full or half empty, it's all full. The part we don't see is full of air, therefore there is no half empty. Everything that happens is seen in wholeness. Even in the worst times in our life, is still that ray of hope. Things seem dark and during these times it's hard to see the light. The light is there it is just not visible to us at the moment. Here is the parable that I also used in "The Pleiadian Papers" that describes this wholeness.

1. There was a poor market owner who lived with his son in a village. He and his son had a small portion of Seaweed to sell, and to use it to grow more of this special Seaweed. This Seaweed was very good. It was so good that the Emperor passed through and offered the man a large sum of money for all the Seaweed. The marketer refused to sell all his Seaweed. That same night, someone robbed him of all his Seaweed.

2. In the morning the villagers gathered around him and said, "How terrible! What a bad thing, you don't have any Seaweed, and you don't have the Emperor's money!"

3. The marketer responded, "Maybe it is bad, maybe it is not. All I know is that all my Seaweed is gone and I don't have the Emperor's money."

4. Days later someone came and returned the Seaweed, there was much more Seaweed than what the marketer owned. They caught the thief that has stolen the Seaweed and he had extra on him.

5. The villagers gather around him and said, "How wonderful! A good thing has happened to you. Soon you will be a wealthy man."

6. The marketer responded and said, "Maybe it's good, maybe it's not. All I know is that I have my Seaweed back and much more."

7. Soon after the return of the Seaweed the marketer's son ate too much Seaweed. He didn't clean it, therefore it made him sick.

8. Again one of the villagers came and said, "What a tragedy that has befallen you! You won't be able to manage this all by yourself, and now you have no one to help you with the business, which will cause great losses, especially when others hear about how your son got very sick from the Seaweed."

9. The marketer said, "Maybe it's bad, maybe it's not. All I know is that my son is ill from the Seaweed."

10. The next day the Emperor returned to the village. This time he was leading his soldiers to a brutal battle that was rounding up new recruits, most of whom would die in battle. Because of his illness, the marketer's son was passed over.

11. This time the villagers, who were full of grief at the loss of their sons, rushed to the marketer and said, "Your son has been spared! You are so blessed! It was a good thing that he got very sick from the Seaweed. Now he will not die like the rest of the boys from the village."

12. The marketer replied, "Maybe it is bad, maybe it is not. All I know is that my son did not have to go join the Emperor in his fight." This story ends here. It could continue on and on. The idea is to treat all external events equally by not adding meaning to each twist and turn that life brings. Everything that happens equal balance. The marketer remains calm while the villagers' emotions are swayed back and forth like a tree branch in a storm. By reacting like the villagers, we waste energy searching for a good thing to counteract the lack of. It is this constant search for external highs, which is fleeting and causes the lows that we feel. Instead realize the wholeness and see that everything equals balance. There is no lack of, everything is there, and we just have to see.

Since feeling good brings healing and breath takes a role in the heart center, I have some exercises that can expand the heart and strengthen your healing process.

In Greek mythology the god Eosphoros also known as Phosphorus which means Light-Bringer which is the Morning Star associated with the planet Venus in its morning appearance. His symbolizes the ruler of the powers of the air, the interface between gods and humans. The inner light. The heart center is associated with the planet Venus and the Christ. In the book of revelations 22.16 in the human bible Jesus is referred to as the Morning Star.

In Greek mythology you can see the symbol as the interface between gods and humans like the heart center is the interface between the lower vortexes and the higher vortexes. Here are some breath techniques that will bring spiritual enlightenment and healing of the body and spirit.

Mediation one: Sit with cross legs, such as half or full lotus position. Have hands rested on knees with palms down. Inhale three times. Turn palms up and then inhale three more times. Pause and inhale five more times. Put your hands before you in what is called in some pagan traditions the Triangle of Manifestation pose (Figure 4.5).

Figure 4.5
The Triangle of Manifestation

Have your hands position about the bridge of your nose level where you can see through the triangle at eye level. While in this position inhale while counting to 60% then hold for 10 seconds and exhale. Again inhale, but this time 80% and hold for 10 seconds. This next time around inhale 40% and hold, and the last one in this exercise is to inhale for 30% and hold and exhale.

With this exercise you will gain control over the energy in the body. Through the subtle conditioning of the mind, body and breath, this will perfect the subconscious regulation of all organic functions.

The element of the heart center is air. Air carries the voice of nature's fury and the calming song of the wind. The wind resides in the nature of change and entropy. Both subtle and potent. In one instant we can focus on security and foundations, where in another instant our energy can spring into having our dreams flight.

When we breathe, air carries oxygen to each cell of our body for renewal. In almost every esoteric tradition breath is used to prepare for mediation. The breath during meditation becomes the guiding light leading to inner worlds where insight and peace reign.

To listen to the voice of the wind, is to learn to listen and tap into the insight and understanding at will. In our soul air becomes the fresh winds that awaken the inner voice.

Breath is the bridge to the universe. Breathing techniques puts one in the moment. Breath like the heart center is the mediator between the body and you. It is also the mediator between you and the Universe. Your body is the manifestation of the universe that came to you, if the mediator between you and your body is broken, and then you die. By mastering your breath you can be in the moment where you will tap into the force of life and transcend time and space.

Each exhale of breath is death and each inhale is rebirth, so with each breath, you are dying and being reborn. When your breath comes in, observe. You will realize for a moment that there is no breath. As the breath comes in there is a point of no breath, then as you exhale, again breath comes to a stop until the next inhale. At the point at the pause between inhale and exhale, you are not breathing and therefore you are not here. You're dead. Since it is so fast, you never realize this rebirthing process.

In our daily lives, we must die daily. We must consciously pay attention to be proactive each day. Each day take action to open your heart. Each day allow yourself to be a better individual than yesterday. This takes effort because we carry our fears and dreams with us and must use conscious effort to see what we can do to make a difference in your life and others. For example pause and perhaps think about what you can do to make someone feel better today. Too many times we get so caught up in our self and our perceived problems that we want to withdrawn, close ourselves off to everywhere. It is so easy to fall into this habit and become self centered. Perhaps make a list of what you can do to reach out and make a difference.

Reiki or healing of hands is due to life force energy and love. To prepare for healing on hands, one must put the ego to the side through affirmation or prayer. This allows one to have love flow through them as life force is directed to the area to be healed. To practice the laying of hands one must have their life in balance as well to heal. The patient that is being healed by Reiki must also be balance by living an ethical life in order to complete the healing so that it doesn't reverse back. Some cases people have been healed by laying of hands and then the illness comes back days later because their mind wasn't right by their lifestyle.

---
---
---
---
---

**Christ Consciousness:** You must acknowledge the wondrous Love that the Universe has for you to allow your experience in the realm of life unfolding. You are the co-creator in the infinity of the Creation that is a manifestation of the Eternal One. Therefore when you despise yourself or another, you despise the very Spirit of Life Eternal which all exists within you.

Of the millions of sensually-dominated humans, those who are controlled by their five senses however, one of them awakens that divine spark which all inherits from the Creation, and becomes an extraordinary human being with extraordinary knowledge and power. We call these great men geniuses.

Genius is the first step away from the purely physical body toward realizes that you are not your body. Every genius has begun to develop God-awareness in him and knows that he is Consciousness and not body.

You must knowingly create yourself and your destiny with the Universe and in accordance with the law of balanced in everything that you do. To work with the Universe knowingly, you must know how the Universe works. You can know the Universe only by knowing yourself as Consciousness instead of thinking of yourself as your body. Opening your heart causes you to realize that your body is just a machine that YOU occupy.

The transition from sensed-body awareness to God-Mind awareness comes to the human race very slowly. It is the sole purpose of these lessons to know Consciousness as the ONE reality and that everything in the universe as a simulation of reality. Man can think only what he knows in his Consciousness, or senses through his body. This same principle also applies to nations. Men and nations become what they think. Their standards are determined by their thinking. Beneficial standards are attained through Higher Self mastery, and chaos is created by reactive thinking based on being a slave to our emotions.

Since we do have a physical body to interact in this physical world which houses your spirit of the God Within, then you must take care of the needs of the body with proper food, water, exercise, shelter, rest so that you can remain vibrant, clean and healthy in order to perform with honor the service of the Universe. Therefore you must love yourself as God and God as Self, which means loving yourself and having unconditional love for others. This is the steps toward achieving Christ Consciousness, recognizing within you the Divine light of the One All That Is.

We as sentient beings are the only animals with the potential of unlimited self-awareness. Meditation is one of the most important of the functions of humanity which causes advance human growth. When we meditate certain chemicals are released in the brain causing us to become more aware of the Source of One. The chemical produced allows us to become more aware of the interconnected Source, very much how the right transistors in a radio pick up waves in the atmosphere.

Meditation can be used to transform your body and life to anyway that one wishes. Meditation is to think inwardly instead of outwardly by depending on the five senses which can be deceptive.

Jesus told man to seek the "kingdom of heaven" within himself, not outside of himself. By that He meant that God dwelt within man, and that God-awareness will come to any man who communes with the Source through inner awareness. Everything that we want and need is inside of us. We tend to get caught up in the illusion of being separate and alone. We feel hurt when needs are not meant. We are a manifestation of the Whole, a fractal that means all the information of the Whole exist within each fractal of existence. The only difference between each fractal is the degrees of self-awareness. Since our potential of self-awareness is unlimited, then we can go inward and find all the information of all existence and realize all is inside us.

Remember the blessings in our lives. We tend to forget about the good things in our lives. Many of the attitude is "What have you done for me lately?" We must remember those blessings as we allow the ray of love to shine through us.

**Empathy:** Empathy is needed for any healthy relationships. Sociopaths totally lack empathy. To understand others and to be able to give others what they need and want, empathy is necessary. If you are having problems in a relationship, imagine being that person and see the world through their eyes. By doing this, you may be surprise on what their needs are and why they are responding the way they are. This allows you to understand the other person better. Empathy is needed to have unconditional love, to be able to relate to others. Allow yourself to see yourself through their eyes. You may see what it is they love about you and perhaps what it is that you need to work on. Realize you are loved and it is not something to be earned. You are love.

Pleiadian Spirals of Light

# THE FIFTH SPIRAL
## (Element *Ether*)

The Fifth spiral of the Power Center is located in the throat area. It is the throat energy center. It is associated with the element Ether. This Power Center is about Communication and creativity. Here is a correspondent of the symbolism of this power center.

**Element:** Sound
**Function:** Communication, creativity
**Glands:** thyroid, parathyroid
**Unbalances:** Sore throats, stiff neck, thyroid problems
**Color:** blue
**Sephira:** Geburah, Chesed

The Fifth Spiral is associated with communication. In this vortex we cross more into the realms of mind and spirit. The throat where the center is located is the passage way of nutrients, breath pass through the neck from the mouth, brain and nose. In this Power Center we find about the truth about the mind. Here we realize that we are not our thoughts, we are not our mind. We are not the words we speak.

This Power Center is married to the Personal Power Center. It is through communication mostly through our mouths that gives us personal power when we express our needs. Through our mouth vibrates sound. The sound we hear is a vibration of air molecules as they are affected by matter in movement. When I speak, the sound that reaches you is from the air I have disturbed. All sound is vibration, and everything, no matter what has its own frequency of sound.

Dr. W.J. John Weilgart allegedly received a language by extraterrestrials called the aUI which translate as the Language of Space. In this language there are 31 elements that represent the most basic and universal categories in all languages. Together they would form the 'periodic table' of the semantic elements of

95

all human thought and expression. The symbols for each element describe the essence, and when created to describe something, the elements that are chosen by the individual are form together to describe the essence of things. In this language the numerical value in the word To Live, Immortal and Word has the same numerical value which is 8.

The Word is the same numerical as to live and Immortal. "In the beginning was the Word, and the Word was with God, and the Word was God. And the Word was made flesh and dwelled among us." Many people think that this just applied to one known as Jesus. The Word brings life and it is also those who take action towards life. When your imagined desires are strong you give life to them, by the gravity force that stimulates electricity that manifest things in the material world. Your desire is spiritual sound that manifests bodies. Sound comes from the movement of manifestation. Desire has a sound. The Immortal is the one who brings life. Not only does he bring life extension to himself, he brings life to all he manifests. The Source itself creates bodies through desire. And then we do the same. The Immortal brings all that he desires to life. He brings life to all those around him. He is the life giver. He does this through his actions of benefiting the human species. When the Word is encircled in space then you have the number 9, which is the Source. It is also the numerical value of the word language of space/ Space Spirit Sound.

The Immortal which is the Word = 8 when the Word/Immortal is encircled within space, then the Immortal is 9 which is the Source.

Above which is 28, when you have Above Immortal that is 28 + 27 + 5 + 21 = 9. That is ktov

Therefore there are many names to call the Source, Such as aUI, ktov, kU. (Space spirit sound, Higher Immortal, Higher Mind/Spirit.) All of these equal 9. The Source is the All That Is, Consciousness , that which is called God.

The universe itself is made of sound. Without sound and language there is no form. Sound creates. That is why this energy center is also associated with creativity. Desire stimulates the vibration. The desire from the Source disturbs the vacuum of space and from that is positive and negative ions which creates electricity. This is created by sound produced from desire that creates a vibration from the disturbance of energy in the vacuum. Electricity then has its own unique sound which again, just like desire (gravity) causes a disturbance which eventually over time gives birth to the atom. Each atom has its own unique vibration of sound.

For this energy center to be plugged in, one must attain a certain level of purification. This purification is needed to have the sensitivity to the higher subtler levels energy centers.

This is also the realm of telepathy. When your throat center is open your abilities of telepathy is increased. On a subconscious level we all communicate to some degree telepathically. When we fulfill our desires or fears, it is due to each of us subconsciously communicating with each other that create synchronicities. Therefore there are no coincidences; all is in synch with our subconscious telepathy.

Since most humans lack certain awareness, when someone consciously uses telepathy on a subject, that subject believes the impulse is his own thoughts. He is unaware that he is picking up a telepathic thought from someone else. The extraterrestrial beings that are advance have the awareness to know where the source of the one who sends the telepathic message. If you make telepathic contact with them, they will know the message came from you. The fifth Kind is when one makes conscious contact with Higher Beings such as extraterrestrials or Ascended Masters which is usually by telepathic means. It is then up to them how and if they wish to respond. Having this awareness gives you a better chance to choose to respond because you know the origin of where the thought came from, other than just reacting on impulse because you think it's originally came from you.

Love which is the mediator between the higher centers and lower centers is the key to telepathy. If you lack love, the telepathic subconscious impulses that you send out are emptiness. This can cause many to be repelled by the telepathic message that is being sent out. If you have muck and garbage inside you, you are only going to attract others with muck and garbage inside them, while you repel those who radiate love. One cannot attract love if they lack love. If an individual is neurotic where they have a low sense of self-worth for example, he/she may try to seek love. While seeking they are telepathically sending out messages to be rejected. The only ones they seem to attract are other neurotics who are rejected so they have something in common as they settle for each other. Neurotics usually find all their friends are also neurotics. Here is an example of how this happens. Tammy has low self worth and tries to make friends to no success. She doesn't know why that is so. She feels lonely and yearns for that contact. Eventually she meets people who accept her and for the first time she feels like she has friends. There is one catch; all of them are drug addicts. Before you know it Tammy is associating with just a bunch of drug addicts, before long Tammy winds up becoming a drug addict. Now as long as she feels she cannot have friends beyond what she attracts at the moment, she will stay trapped. Even though Tammy didn't start out as a drug user, why did she just attract drug addicts? The reason why is because what she and the drug addicts did have in common was their view of low self worth. To have healthy people be attracted to you, you first have to be healthy yourself. Using telepathy or a spell to attract someone is not going to do much good if you do not love yourself. The spell may work, but the results will only be temporally. Instead one has to love themselves and then they will spark loving feelings from those others. Working on yourself, then it will last.

There is one Light and we are all a part of it. Everything affects the whole. Prayer is a form of telepathy. We have the ability to heal at a distance. When an individual or group of people pray for someone those healing thoughts are sent to the receiver which influences him subconsciously and heals him, the more participants, the stronger the telepathic messages. Since there is only one Light no matter when and where the individuals are that are praying those messages are sent out like ripples affecting the whole. When it comes to anything, the more people who believe in something, the more they send out telepathic messages that influence those who will make that belief a reality. Not only does talking about good things that happen to you cause good feelings that help create an increase of those good things. Also talking about good things also causes the listeners to believe that good things happen to you. When those listeners believe this, their combine subconscious telepathy influences you on a telepathic level where you believe it more yourself, therefore feeding your good feelings aid in you into having an increase of good things happening to you.

Sometimes which first started as a lie, can be made into truth if you get enough people to believe it's true. Example, Heinrich Khunrath created an allegory or hoax about a mystic named Christian Rosenkreuz who studied in the Middle East under different masters such as the Sufi, and from that he founded the Rosicrucian Order. This was written in the *Fama Fraternitatis*. During this time, there was no Rosicrucian Order, but because so many people believe that this Order did exist, it became a reality. Today the Rosicrucian Order exists with teachings that originally come from ancient Egyptian Mysteries schools.

Therefore by telling someone to expect something with enough conviction, where they completely believe you, their receptive minds will project the event to happen. If someone wants to believe you bad enough, they will send telepathic energies that will manifest the energy, for example to heal.

Faith healers do this; many miracles are performed in this manner. They say something will happen, and the mass consciousness creates the outcome. This mass consciousness projects ripples out throughout the one Light and all those individuals who will play a part into making it manifest will be there at the exact time to play their part in manifesting what is expected to occur.

What happens if you go to sleep with bad feelings? Most likely you will have nightmares. The characters in your dream are all a creation of how you felt. If you feel like a victim, in the nightmare that is what you will be. This law doesn't just apply in your sleep; you also attract the people in your life that reflects how you feel.

Therefore be cautious of what you say or write to others. What you fear, is best to not speak and let die in your mind. Speaking those fears will only amplify them, while those who listen, their thoughts may add to its manifestation while you feel more fearful for just talking about it.

Therefore it's best to speak only about what you want to happen. What you speak and write to others, their minds will help manifest it.

Tell others what you anticipate that which what you want. Show them how it will come to pass. Your words to others will increase many times with each new mind accepting your words. Know who you are talking to as well. Some people by telling them what success you will have may cause doubt. If many you told have doubt, then their combined doubts will hinder you and add to your failure. Therefore in this case 'silence is golden.' One must make sure the circles of people you discuss what you will accomplish are people who are headed that way. Telling pessimistic people or people who lost faith in you will only add to your struggle. If you tell one person who doesn't believe you and he/she tells others about your silly fantasies, you will have the one you told plus the others that he told negative thoughts going against your dream. You will be outnumbered.

Each mind that accepts what you say will multiply, not add the power of that manifestation that will come. Therefore be careful what you say and "Do not Cast your pearls before swine for they will trample on them and tear you apart," Four people's pessimistic thoughts going against your dream is just as powerful as four people who pray to heal someone. The pessimistic people may not be on their knees wishing you to fail, but their negative doubts alone will be the fuel. FBI Carl Hanratty told Frank Abagnale Jr. in the movie "Catch me if You Can" based on a true story that he will catch him because it is a mathematical fact. That is because even though Abagnale had the desire to get away,

Hanratty has a team of FBI helping him. The FBI's desired minds outweighs Abagnale's mind. Each FBI agent's mind multiplies the desire to catch him. This is why it is a mathematical fact that Frank Abagnale got caught. The more minds that agree with your dream, the better the results. Since all is one Light, whatever you speak to another you speak to the Light. It is the Light which shall bring forth those dreams, the God within each individual. The Light is the All That Is.

**Telepathy experiment:** There may have been times that the phone rang and you knew who it was without looking at your caller ID. You may have known what someone was about to say. Here is an experiment to try. Have you and another face each other. Have a note book. Gaze into their eyes or you can close your eyes. Visualize a picture or use words. They will respond to your telepath thought that you projected. Write the first thing that comes to mind. Have the other do the same.

Another exercise is to face seated opposite each other. Taste something without the other knowing it. Except that this is a psychic taste. Focus on placing what you tasted upon the tongue of the receiver. The receiver will let you know as soon as he tastes it.

**Sounds:** Certain syllables also have effect upon our body. The ancient Tibetan mantra "Om mani padme hum" is the sound manifestation of pure compassion. This sound brings peaceful vibrations that give serenity and joy. In Hebrew the sound "Amen" at the end of prayer is similar to the Om sound. In Hebrew there is no e in the sound. It was originally Amn. In Sanskrit it's 'Aum" instead of 'Om." Om is the matrix of all sounds and gives rise to all words in all languages. Aum/Om has a threefold division of time.

A – is the waking state
U – is the dream state
M – is the state of deep sleep

The pause at the end of the sound is infinite consciousness. At the end of Amn, the n is the completion, the infinite circle. Om is the sound of creation; it also stimulates the rise of the energy force in our astral body. When we say the mantra Om/Aum, the A sound starts in the heart center and the U is in the throat center and the M is at the Third Eye (Figure 5.1). Therefore the Om sound takes our focus to the Third Eye.

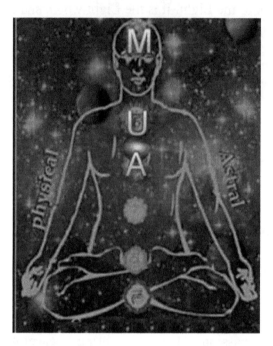

Figure 5.1
Om/Aum effect on body

The Music of the Spheres or Word goes beyond the spoken language. There is a Sacred Sound which correlates to "Om" and the Sufi "HU". The Word is also called the Sound of God or Breath of God since all sound permeates all things, as all things is made of energy as all matter breathes in and out in a rhythm.

This sound current that permeates all is the connecting link between the Divine and man. This divine current is always playing a symphony of ethereal music. One cannot hear it until they progress enough spiritually to hear it in the inner ear. Many

Pleiadian Spirals of Light

mystics during meditation have seen different colors with their inner eye.
All the manifestations of the Light have a different sound. Here is a list on each Hz on the vibrational manifestation of different frequencies. This is an electric wave universe that continuously gives birth to different manifestations of itself. With each new birth there is a corresponding sound that goes with it.

| | |
|---|---|
| Gamma Rays | $10^{\wedge}18$ to $10^{\wedge}26$hz |
| X rays | $10^{\wedge}16$ to $10^{\wedge}20$hz |
| Ultraviolet Light (UV) | $10^{\wedge}15$ to $10^{\wedge}17$hz |
| Visible Light | $10^{\wedge}4.7$ to $10^{\wedge}15$hz |
| Infrared Rays | $10^{\wedge}11$ to $10^{\wedge}4.7$hz |
| Radar Waves | $10^{\wedge}9.5$ to $10^{\wedge}11.5$hz |
| Microwaves | $10^{\wedge}8$ to $10^{\wedge}9.5$hz |
| Television Waves | $10^{\wedge}6$ to $10^{\wedge}8$hz |
| Radio Waves | $10^{\wedge}1$to $10^{\wedge}6.5$hz |
| Elf Waves | $10^{\wedge}1$hz |

Earths Ionosphere Cavity Resonance – Schuman Field ranges from 1 Hz to 30 Hz – Radiation Spectrum

| | |
|---|---|
| Audio20 | 20,000 Hz |
| Ultrasonic | 20,000 Hz – 100-kHz – 10 MHz |
| Radiofrequency | 150KHz-1.5 MHz |
| High Radio Frequency RF | 1.5MHz-40 MHz |
| Very High Radio Frequency VHF | 40MHz-100MHz |

| Ultrahigh Radio Frequency UH | over 100MHz |
|---|---|

Molds, viruses, bacteria, worms, mites range from 77 KHz to 900KHz

| Warts | 400-430Kz |
|---|---|
| Tapeworms | 420-450Khz |
| Mites | 640KHz – 850KHz |
| Ant | 1000 to 1200KHz |
| Goldfish | 900 to 1500Khz |
| Chameleon | 1000 to 6000KHz |
| Cat | 1500 to 8000Khz |
| Human Body Cell | 1,520,000 to 9,460,000 Hz |
| Upper Limit of Human Hearing | 15,000 Hz |

Sounds can have an effect on things and people. Extremely low frequency (ELF) have been said to have ecological impact and perhaps long term occupational exposure to Alzheimer's disease. There are other speculations by conspiracy theorist, but I won't go into that.

Tests have shown how different frequencies of Hz affect us. Our brain has basically five states of frequencies, which are alpha activity (8–12 Hz) that can be detected from the occipital lobe during the time of relaxed while awake and increases when the eyes are closed. Other frequency bands are: delta (1–4 Hz), theta (4–8 Hz), beta (13–30 Hz) and gamma (30–70 Hz). EEG signals change dramatically during sleep and show a transition from faster frequencies to increasingly slower frequencies such as alpha waves.

Many tribes in their ceremonies beat drums. The beating of drums and the flickering of the fire puts our mind in altered states of consciousness. Today we have devices called Brainwave Entrainments that causes brainwave synchronization which occurs when the "right brain" and "left brain" work in a deep partnership with each other. Brainwave Entrainment produces binaural beats that affect our minds to a more degree than the sound of drums. When binaural beats in both ears and the combination is 4-8Hz your brain waves are altered and will go into a theta state, which is the realm of creative thought and insightful breakthroughs come from. This is also the state of deep mediation.

Brainwave Entrainment can put your mind in different states of meditation just by the binaural beats and lights that flicker in harmony with it. What takes years of meditation to reach certain states, Brainwave Entrainment can take you there right away without any skill in mediation at all. When listening to the beats your brain waves are adjusted internally and then synchronize with the external cycle of sound waves.

The binaural beats into our ears, they send sound waves to our brain. Our brain waves listen to the sounds, and start to follow the pace and rhythm of them. The act of entraining brain waves increases production of "feel good chemicals" in the body; anxiety levels go down and happiness goes up; sleep is improved; mood improves; and you become more relaxed. Binaural beats can get you into this state quicker than anything else on the planet! Therefore Brain Entrainment causes instant meditation.

**Meditation:** Meditation is one of the most important things needed in order to grow spiritually. Each time that you meditate you send out love. When you send out love, more love comes back to you. Meditation is a form of communication. When you meditate you allow yourself to listen to the Divine. You then open yourself up to allowing the God within you to work knowingly through you. You then become a channel for the Divine to work through you where inspiration and ideas just flow to you.

Through meditation you can create anything or be what you want. The more that you mediate the more that you realize the Oneness of all things. You begin to realize that separation is nothing but an illusion. Through meditation you can communicate to the subconscious to heighten any skills or abilities that you want. You can program your subconscious to fulfill your desires. You can ask questions. Sometimes the answer may come in a flash, or sometimes it comes later through circumstances or other people.

Meditation as I said earlier can also be used to telepathically communicate with advanced Beings. One can receive information telepathically from advance races from other worlds. The information can come as an impulse or feeling or desire to create something. Some may ask, why communicate with other beings when you can just communicate with the God within? When you are meditating you are communicating with the God within, sometimes we may have to receive answers through other people when we are not sensitive as yet to the direct source. Those other people can be Highly advance beings, or daily situation that lead us to a ordinary human being that gives us the answer. You may turn on the television and lo and behold the answer may be what someone says on the screen. Sometimes we need that nudge to confirm what the God within has told us that we may question or not be able to hear.

Some people after having contact with extraterrestrial beings develop a certain skill. The Beings have the ability to trigger certain abilities in people. They may communicate by guiding the human into projecting that skill, and by repetition the human learns to harness that skill on his own. Uri Geller claims after his contact with a Being in a garden he developed telekinetic ability. He also said the Beings worked through him in some demonstrations and even teleported him.

Pastor Wesley Henry says that after he encountered the angel Gabriel he started having premonitions about the future. His mental state was healed and his IQ also increased. Billy Meir also developed premonitions after his encounters with Beings.

Michael Tolbot says that after he encountered a mysterious Woman in White that appeared with a Man in Black after a UFO, he started developing Involuntary Subliminal Psychokinesis (ISP). He witness poltergeist activity in his home and believes that ISP is the source of the phenomenon. He believes that his encounter somehow triggered that ability within him.

Many times Higher Beings have triggered astral projection. Many witnesses have been pulled out of their body when one or more of the Beings were around.

I had my own personal experience years ago. Years ago I was over my best friend's apartment. She told me good night and went into her bedroom. Just as I lay on the couch before my head can even barely touch the pillow I felt an electric current in my mouth and suddenly I find myself traveling in a tunnel of light. My first response was that I was frightened by this. To comfort myself, I called upon Jesus and then I started flying even faster through the tunnel of light. I was moving at enormous speed and suddenly I am back on the couch. As I looked around, I saw that I am back in the living room I felt a female presence and smelled perfume and a name of this entity and a message suddenly came to me. Years later when I saw the movie "Contact" starring Jodi Foster I saw the wormhole she traveled in and realize it looked exactly identical to the tunnel of light I was flying through.

Since our potential of self-awareness is unlimited that means all the information of the Source is in everything and that is within us, therefore we have the potential to access all the knowledge of God within. Meditation is the desire to become one with God within. God's knowledge is asleep within you and all of it can be awakened. The Third Eye which is discussed more in the next chapter is about seeing through God's eye. God's mind is your mind. This is perfect communion. With each communion with the Divine you get more knowledge as the God within touches the Universal Source.

**Telepathic Placebo Effect:** The placebo is Latin for "I shall please." It is an ineffectual medical treatment for a disease in order to deceive the patient into thinking the medicine is authentic. Sometimes when the patient is given the placebo they have an improvement in their medical condition. The amazing thing is that the placebo effect is more powerful when the doctor is also deceived into believing that the medicine is real. That is because of the power effect of two minds believing that the drug is real, therefore on a subconscious level the doctor and patient use their minds to heal the illness within the patient. When the doctor knows it's a placebo and the patient doesn't know, the effect isn't as powerful since it's just up to the patient alone to heal themselves. Sometimes the doctor's pessimism will get in the way of the placebo where he telepathically puts a suggestion of doubt within the patient. The placebo effect cures 1/3 of all illnesses. That means a large amount of health problems can be cured by our mind.

The mind is powerful to the point that even people with multiple personalities can change eye color, turn off/on allergies, and even have multiple menstruation cycles for each personality. On a sci-fi show called Forever Knight a vampire had a split personality. While one personality believed that she was human, she was able to go out into the sunlight and eat human food as vampire she could not. Even though this show is science fiction it demonstrates the power of the mind.

Under hypnosis people can control heart rate, body temperature, visual acuity, and will away scars and birthmarks. Grigori Yefimovich known as Rasputin used the power of the mind to influence little Alexei Romanov blood to clot in his condition of hemophilia. Rasputin was skilled in hypnosis and was very good in the power of suggestion.

A subject named Jack Schwartz conducted by D. Elmer Green at the Menninger Institute in Kansas demonstrated great feats such as pressing a lit cigarette to his skin for twenty seconds without any harm to his skin. Green reported that Schwartz put his hands into a large brazier of burning coal and grabbed a handful of burning coals as he walked around the room. As he dropped the coals into newspaper the paper burst into flames.

Here is what Michael Talbot quoted in his book the Holographic Universe. *"Even surgery has been used as a placebo. In the 1950s, angina pectoris, recurrent pain in the chest and left arm due to decreased blood flow to the heart, was commonly treated with surgery. Then some resourceful doctors decided to conduct an experiment. Rather than perform the customary surgery, which involved tying off the mammary artery, they cut patients open and then simply sewed them back up again. The patients who received the sham surgery reported just as much relief as the patients who had the full surgery."*
There have been awesome results in hypnosis as well that shows the interconnectivity of the mind. The hypnotist hypnotized a subject to jump every time he touches his tie, even when the subjects back was turned or in another room he still responded to the suggestion. Consciously he would have no way of knowing when the hypnotist randomly touched his tie, but he responded anyway.
Calvin Hall of the University of Virginia did an experiment in dream telepathy. The subject was told to pantomime a randomly selected scene and think, feel and act the scene out. Hall also added a twist. Some of the subjects knew they were in a telepathy study while others thought they were in a sleep study. Hall realized that 29 of the 36 cases of the direct pantomime were included in the subjects' dreams. This happen even when they didn't know they were in a telepathy study. So even with the lack of knowledge that they will receive a message in a dream didn't make a difference. Research has shown that while sleeping the average person has the telepathic sensitivity equal to that of a psychic.
In Quantum Physics there is a phenomenon called Quantum Entanglement where two or more particles such as photons, electrons, interact with each other, once separate no matter the distance as one particle is effected the other one no matter the distance is effected too. This quantum entanglement is how telepathy works. Everything is one Light and separation is just an illusion.

Sometimes partners or twins have sympathetic pains or illnesses. Identical twins named Bobbie and Betty were almost always together. Bobbie was the dominant twin while Betty would experience Bobbie's thoughts. When Bobbie became ill, Betty was ill to. When both became schizophrenia they were committed to a state hospital. When they failed to improve within a year they was separated and placed in different wings of the hospital so that they couldn't communicate with each other.

One spring night the head nurse found Bobbie dead. When the nurse decided to check on Betty she was dead as well. Both were found dead on the floor in a fetus position lying on their right side.

Telepathy can also be used to glamour. Many probably heard this term on the HBO series True Blood. I am not talking about this advance level of glamour where the vampires have the ability to erase memories and compel others to do your bidding. There are advance humans such as the Ascended Masters and extraterrestrials who have that ability. Look how many abductees forget about their experiences. Even though this is possible, I am talking about a lesser degree. When detectives use disguises to deceive it takes more than just altering the physical appearance. One must mentally mask themselves of their true identity. They have to feel the part they are playing to such a degree so that others don't pick up a vibe of their true identity. This glamour is used to deceive others into believing that you really are the role that you are portraying. You have to be convinced yourself to give off the vibe that you want.

Some of the advance extraterrestrials use this ability to give the contactee the vibe they wish the contactee will perceive. Whitley Streiber encountered a extraterrestrial and the vibe perception that Streiber got was that the visitor was a vampire. This inspired him to write the vampire series novels such as The Hunger and Lilith's dream. They could have hid this from him if they wanted to, but they wanted this message passed on to him.

When I was just getting out of high school I accidently used glamour when I walked into a Christian bookstore. That day I was

110

feeling in synch with an alien presence after watching one of my favorite shows. When I walked into the Christian bookstore the first impression that the clerk received was that I was an angel disguised as a human. She was even more shocked when I grabbed a book on angels just as she predicted. While looking through the book, she and her friend excused me and told me what they thought and was concerned. After asking me twenty questions they realize I was human just like them, but became afraid because my ideas of God and the universe didn't fit their ideas.

Therefore glamour works, look at the actors on movies, a good actor can make you temporally forgot who is playing the part, so just imagine good acting with a good disguise.

**Personal Power;** Every energy center except the heart center is paired with another center. The three lower centers are married to the three higher centers. The third spiral the personal power center is married to the throat center for the voice is where we gain our personal power.

Through communication is how we advance our career and personal life. We know what we say is important and speak to get our needs met. With a strong throat center your communication skills are strong. The quiet nice guy/girl doesn't just struggle in the area of their personal life; they usually struggle in all areas. The nice guy/girl is the one who works at a job for years and never get a raise.

The problem is they are not seeing the value of themselves so others don't either. In all relationships, business or romantic it all comes down to "what's in it for me." This may sound selfish, but it is the nature of humans. When you go to buy a car you get the one that will do the best for you. If the salesman tried to sale you a car by convincing you that he needs to sell one to have money to take care of his family, you are not going to care. Instead you would feel insulted. This would be the same if you tried to be in a romantic relationship by trying to convince the other you need them. Just like you wouldn't buy a car unless it's one that you want, you are not going to partner with anyone romantic unless you see that you are getting something out of it.

One will not do business with someone unless it's something in it for them. Therefore to be a business partner or romantic partner with someone you have to present yourself as the best commodity that they can get. Everyone has a market value and you must set yourself as a good catch. The problem with the quiet nice guy/girl is that they have low value of themselves and think they have nothing value to say and believe they won't get their needs met anyways. This erroneous thinking mostly starts in the formative years of our life when we cry to get our needs met while our parent isn't responding. When this happens, early we think; what's the point of expressing ourselves when our needs won't get met anyway. All this causes is built up anger making us feel depressed while our life seems shitty.

As I mentioned previously about glamour, people see us the way we see ourselves. If you want to excel in your career or have someone fall in love with you, you must convince them that they are getting a good deal working or being with you. To do that you must convince yourself that you have something to offer that is valuable.

This usually happens on a subconscious level, but science has confirmed that marketing principles apply to all types of relationships. In romantic relationships for example, lovers unconsciously calculate the other person's comparable worth, hidden costs and assumed depreciation of the relationship. They ask themselves, "Is this the best deal I can get?"

Even though love is about sharing, sacrifice and giving, this happens after one falls in love. In the beginning it's about what in it for them. In the case with sociopaths since they lack empathy and are narcissistic they do not develop feelings toward the people they use, any more than they do with a toy. They also choose a partner for the same reason as "what's in it for me," the difference is in a healthy relationships both partners empathize and know what to give the other to keep them happy. With sociopaths it's only a one way deal. They don't care what your needs are nor can empathize to even fulfill them. Therefore sociopaths make their partners feel short changed. Once they have no more use for them they throw them away like an old toy.

In a regular relationship when we see that partner is no longer providing our needs we do this on a subconscious level, but because of empathy normal people usually don't toss someone to the side like garbage. They break up with them in the most respectable way they know how. The sociopath is the con artist that gives you false promises and never fulfills them. This is when victims feel used. In any business transaction and other relationships both parties are unconsciously using each other, but since it's a mutual agreement where both parties are getting their needs met, no one feels used. It is just like a business transaction in a store. If you are getting what you paid for, then you are ok with giving your money to the salesman. If the salesman doesn't give you what you paid for, you will feel short changed. This also applies in any relationship.

The individual whose throat center is strong will use these tactics in every type of relationship. He/she will convince their boss that they are a good commodity in the business, and giving them a raise will benefit his company. They will convince their desired business partner that having them as their partner will help them succeed. Barnes did this to convince Thomas Edison to be his business partner. In the beginning Edison thought Barnes was just a tramp. Barnes convinced him otherwise. Everyone wants the best deal possible in life and also in love. Research have shown that the more qualities you bring to the bargaining deal, the better chances you will do in all aspects, including love.

There are certain qualities to have to upgrade yourself for others to see you as a catch. Some would argue that looks have nothing to do with it. The facts are that people judge by appearance. If you walk into a business wearing street clothes with messed up hair going for a job interview, you are hardly not going to get hired unless you have some other high skills to make up for your physical appearance. In the business world, physical appearances help as well as knowledge, personality and your inner nature. Your associates feel comfortable if you are also dressed similar, are trusted as well as have something to offer. In romantic relationships, it may take a few more traits, such as, physical appearance, money or possessions, status, knowledge, personality and your inner nature.

When it comes to the physical, people are attracted to each other on the similar attractiveness level. There is a balance factor that goes with this. If you want a beauty queen, and you look like a bloated ogre then you better have one of those other traits that stands out to make up for your looks. Observe and you will see most couples appearances are pretty much on the same level. On those rare cases where a beauty queen is with an older not so good looking man, he usually makes it up by his money or status. When a handsome guy is with a girl who doesn't look like much, it may be because she has something else about her that makes her special.

Some may argue that to base someone on looks, prestige and money is being shallow. It's shallow only when you refuse to give that person a chance and refuse to look at his/her other traits based on lack of one trait. The facts are that unconsciously all these factors count. When you buy a car, you are going to want the one that looks good. If the car doesn't appear that physically pleasing to the eye, the only other reason you would buy it is that the car runs exceptionally good and runs better than the other ones on the lot. At the same time we don't want to be caught driving a car that looks like crap. It is the same with people; we don't want to be out with our arm hanging on to someone who literally looks like they climbed out the gutter with an unkempt matted wig with their thong visible with hairy legs and hair sticking out of the crack of their butt cheeks.

People are happier when there is the balance factor. Going after someone who is filthy rich or drop-dead gorgeous might not last as long as someone that is more balanced to your level, as the saying goes, water seeks its own level. Therefore if you want a great man, then you first have to be a great woman. This also applies to the man as well. If you don't follow the balance factor and partner with someone on a different level after the first wave of love wears off, the one who settled will start looking around seeing that he/she deserves better. The other one will feel insecure and worried.

Since physical appearance makes a difference, glamour can be used to make others think you look better. Having a smile on your face with confidence can make a big difference. Having your shoulders back and chest out with a smile can increase your looks. On the other hand, looking miserable and withdrawn can make you look homely looking. The actress Angela Bettis may look plain looking, when she played Carrie White in the first remake of Carrie, she looked very homely looking as her posture had her shoulders forward with her head slightly down without eye contact. When Angela isn't acting homely she is pretty.

Convince yourself that you are the most beautiful person who walked the planet then move in synch with it. Therefore change your body language to seem more appealing. Men move with self assurance with smooth bold movements. Women like a man with some swagger.

Stand before a mirror and observe your posture. Maybe you are slouching. Maybe you're too tense. Look at yourself and have an air of confidence, look manly.

Another thing you can do to rate yourself is look at yourself in the mirror. Rate what number you are within the 10$^{th}$ range. After that, rate the person that you wish to be with. If you are only two points different at the maximum, then you are still within the balance factor and go for it. If your rate is more than that, then you are out of the balance factor and would be wasting your time.

Your tone of voice and the words that you choose also makes a difference in how others see you. Using euphemisms cause others to see you as low class. Those of the upper class call it as it is. When upper class individuals mention about the family jewels, they are talking about the jewels in the safe hidden in the wall. They do not use euphemisms like pussy and dick; instead they call it vagina and penis. They call it like it is. Your tone of voice to present yourself of that of the upper class is to keep your voice low, slower and pronounce all of the syllables and finish every word that comes out of your mouth. Don't cut your words short. Speaking too fast with pressured speech will put others on the defense to block what you have to say. This pressured speech is usually due to one being desperate to be heard. They subconsciously fear that if they do not get it out fast enough to what they want to express then they will be cut off before they are even heard. Speaking loud also cause others to view you as low class and uncouth.

To be effective in the throat center, it is important to be stable in the previous lower energy centers. That is to first be secured financially and being able to stand on both feet on the ground. Financial security only comes from legitimate income. Struggling with money or relying on illegitimate money is not being stably grounded. Money made by illegitimate means can be taken at any time, that is why individuals who do never have enough. Relying on a crutch, one cannot feel the confidence that is a necessity. When you recognize the God within, then you can stand on your own two feet. To acknowledge the God within, you first have to love yourself. Love is the glue that connects all the energy centers. To stand on your own two feet requires willpower. The will is to be exercised daily and achieving material dreams are side effects of realizing the God Within, those side effects are just confirmation of your Oneness with the Source, that you are God.

# THE SIXTH SPIRAL
## (Element *Light*)

The Sixth spiral of the Second Sight Center is located between the eyebrows. It is the center of the Third Eye. It is associated with the element Light. This Power Center is about Knowing. Here is a correspondent of the symbolism of this power center.

**Element:** Light
**Function:** Seeing, intuition
**Glands:** Pineal
**Unbalances:** Nightmares, blindness, headaches
**Color:** Indigo
**Sephira:** Binah, Chokmah

The Third Eye is about intuition. When this energy center is strong you have the intuition to make the right decisions about the choices in your life. You make intuitive decisions about your career and see the intentions of other people. You know things without knowing how you knew them. You may even develop Second Sight where you see future events before they happen, you develop precognition. You also have a clear vision of exactly where you are going and where your life is headed. Second Sight is also called clairvoyance. There are different forms of clairvoyance that you may develop. That is to see into the future, remote viewing where you can see things without being there, and also x-ray clairvoyance where you can see through solid objects.

**The Winged Orb:** The Egyptian symbol of the winged orb (Figure 6.1) is associated with the Third Eye. With intuition we can see through all situations. We see things at a bird's eye view which is seeing the bigger picture. One then sees beyond the physical realm allowing our spirit to fly to distant time and places. The winged orb is also on the caduceus (Figure 6.2).

Pleiadian Spirals of Light

When the two energy poles that intertwine rise up the spine they meet at the Third Eye where the wings are spread. This can also symbolize the cycle of manifestation of dematerialization and remateralization. On a television screen for example the film changes every $30^{th}$ of a second giving us the illusion of motion. Perhaps in the world we live in we materialize and dematerialize even faster. The material world around disintegrates and materializes simultaneously that it happens so fast that our physical eyes cannot see what is really taking place. This constant death and rebirth flow gives us the illusion of movements like images on the film give the illusion of movement on the screen.

Figure 6.1
Egyptian Winged orb

Figure 6.2
Caduceus

As you may realize the caduceus was talked about in the second chapter called The Second Spiral. The reason is that the second energy center which is the sacral center is married to the Third Eye center.

The caduceus symbolizes harmony and balance. In Sumer the twin serpents intertwine symbolized fertility, wisdom and healing. It is a symbol of spiritual awakening and in India it's associated with the Kundalini serpents in Hindu mysticism.

This symbol is used as a symbol of health in medical field because health is about balance. When the energy poles are balance while traveling up the back, it brings health and the awakening of the Third Eye. The winged orb at the top of the caduceus wings are spread so that you can soar beyond what is just right in front of you.

Sex force is the creative force and spiritual awakening is the ability to command. Sex is the power behind force and motion. The sex principle is what causes the uniting of the polarities of electricity and magnetism. All motion from the beginning is spiral and as gravity pulls in representing one polarity, simultaneously radiates outward representing the opposite polarity. The polarity that is drawn inward is electric and is male. The polarity that radiates outward is magnetic and is female. The electric moves counterclockwise as the female moves clockwise and we only see the male polarity as the female is invisible to our eyes. The two are in union which is the one. Nothing can exist without the sex principle of desire. All form is caused by the balance of the two polarities. Everything has both polarities but dominated more in one. That which is dominated as male polarity also has female polarity. That which is dominantly female polarity also has male polarity. The Chinese Taoist symbol Yin/Yang (Figure 6.3) clearly demonstrates this. In the symbol, the white dot within the black swirl is the seed of male within the female (negative). The black dot within the swirl of white is the seed of female within the male (positive) polarity.

**Winged Serpent:** The winged serpent is also a symbol associated with the sixth energy center. The winged serpent has been seen on uniforms of some extraterrestrials (Figure 6.4).

Figure 6.3
Yin Yang symbol used in Taoism.

Figure 6.4
Winged Serpent emblem on Reptoids

The winged serpent has also been seen in many cultures on this earth. In the Mayan culture Quetzalcoatl symbolizes the winged serpent. The winged serpent is a symbol of enlightened consciousness. To be enlightened is to have foresight. To have foresight is to be proactive. Proactive is to create a situation by making something happen instead of life happening to you. Therefore we must move from someone who is affected by everything that happens to them to someone who chooses their experiences. When we move from being proactive to reactive we experience life as something that happens to us. We feel like victims to circumstances and other people. What happened in the past is the past, and one must let go of the past and move forward by creating the life that they want.

The winged serpent shows that human consciousness is created to soar above what's happening on the earth instead of enmeshed in it. Since we have the potential of unlimited Self-Awareness like God then our duty is to be proactive daily to soar higher each day to commune closer to God. Communion closer to God is becoming more aware of who you really are. Seeing your true Self is to see through the Eye of God.

**Eye in the Triangle:** The Third Eye is the eye of God, and the eye in the triangle is the Eye of Providence which is the all seeing eye of God. The symbol is usually an eye with rays of light shining from it inside a triangle (Figure 6.5). Sometimes it is viewed as the eye of God watching over mankind. The most notice of this symbol is on the reverse of the Great Seal of the United States. The Christian Eye of Providence triangle is seen as the Christian Trinity and that the Eye is the all Seeing Eye of God. The seventeenth century showed the Eye of Providence sometimes surrounded by clouds or sunburst.

Figure 6.5
The Christian version
of the Eye of Providence

The Eye of Providence is similar to the Eye of Horus (Figure 6.6) in Egyptian mythology. It is an ancient Egyptian symbol of protection, royal power and good health. The eye is personified as the goddess Udjat which one of the serpents of on the caduceus symbolizes which is a polarity of the energy in the body. Udjat means risen one as in the cobra rising up to protect. Modern occultist adopted the symbol by placing the Eye of Horus inside a triangle. (Figure 6.7) In occult tradition the triangle symbolizes the magic of fire. Horus is the hawk headed god, the Crowned and Conquering Child, which is characterized by growth in consciousness, love and self-actualization.

Figure 6.6
Eye of Horus

Figure 6.7
Modern Occult Eye of Horus inside triangle

Horus is the sun god in Egyptian pantheon. Isis gave birth to a divine son after she fled to the Nile Delta marshlands to hide from her brother Set who wanted to kill her son. Due to the parallel to Horus, Jesus birthday was chosen on the Winter Solstice like Horus and all other sun gods. Horus birth was by divine intervention which was by the golden phallus of Osiris.

The Eye of Providence has been adopted on the reverse side of the Great Seal of the United States in the year 1782. On the seal the words that surround the Eye is Annuit Cœptis which means "He approves our undertakings," Novus Ordo Seclorum means New Order of the Ages. The truncated Pyramid which has deep occult meanings has thirteen steps which represent the original thirteen states and the future growth of the country. The combine implication of this means that God, favors the prosperity of the United States.

Fourteen years after the design on the Seal, the Freemasons adopted their symbol of the Eye of Providence (Figure 6.8). Sometimes the Eye of Providence used in Freemasonry has a semi-circular glory below the eye. Sometimes the Eye is enclosed inside a triangle. Conspiracy theorists believe that it's proof that the Freemasons are behind the Great Seal of the United States, when actually freemasons had nothing to do with the development of the Seal. Benjamin Franklin was the only Freemason involved and his design was shut down. The Freemasons didn't have their symbol until 1797 which is 14 years later after the design on the reverse side of the Great Seal. The Eye of Providence meaning to the Freemasons is the All-seeing God is a reminder that a mason's thoughts and deeds are always seen by God who the masons call the Great Architect of the Universe.

Figure 6.8
Freemasons Eye of Providence

The Great Seal that is used today on the back of the dollar bill wasn't put on currency until the year 1935 by Roosevelt suggested by the Secretary of Agriculture Henry Wallace.

On the website http://www.noahide.org/ there is a picture with the Eye of Providence (Figure 6.9) and here is part of what is written on it. "Within you is the Eye that sees all, inside your brain is a triangular lobe that gathers all that you see, whether you consciously know it or not. All this information is stored in your memory and joins everything you hear within your unconscious mind. These shape your desires, motivations and actions. What you focus on affects your behavior. What you hear influences your judgment. You see all and hear all. Therefore what you choose to see and hear affects your soul..."

By the Grace of G-d.

# WITHIN YOU IS THE EYE THAT SEES ALL.

Inside your brain is a triangular lobe that gathers all that you see, whether you consciously know it or not. All this information is stored in your memory and joins everything you hear within your unconscious mind. These shape your desires, motivations and actions. What you focus on affects you behavior. What you hear influences your judgement. You see all and hear all. Therefore, what you choose to see and hear affects your soul. To be kind, observe kindness in others. To love, see love around you. We are created in the Image and Likeness of the Divine Eyes that see and hear all. As the Torah says, "...0-d saw everything that he had made, and, behold. It was very good." If we see this goodness in everything that 0-d made, so too, will we be as good as 0-d sees us.

KEEP THE SEVEN LAWS ALIVE. BE A CHILD OF NOAH.
www.noahide.org

Figure 6.9

Therefore certain actions are required to open the Eye. We can choose what we see and hear in order for us to shape our desires. A Seer is one who can foretell future events. To be a Seer isn't just about precognition future events. A Seer also creates the future that they want. The Third Eye has a twofold nature which is to perceive and command. We can receive images through perception and also create images to create our reality through visualization. To hold an image in our mind increases the possibility that it will manifest.

**Lucid Dreaming:** Lucid dreaming is being aware that you are dreaming. When you are aware that you are dreaming, then you can have conscious control of your dreams. Conscious control of lucid dreaming, one can foretell future events more easily. In the state of lucid dreaming one can access psychic phenomena. Lucid dreaming also allows you to have mastery in your dreams. The feeling of having mastery in your dreams is carried over to your waking life. Whatever feelings that you have when you go to sleep will determine what you dream. If you go to sleep with bad feelings, you will most likely have a nightmare. This also happens in reverse. If you are having a nightmare, you are most likely going to wake up with bad feelings. The saying 'waking up on the wrong side of the bed" is due to one waking up with bad feelings that they carry with them during the day. Due to the bad feelings one tends to experience unfortunate things throughout the day because the experiences are a reflection of what they feel. They wake up feeling like a victim, and then experience victimization in their daily life. Lucid dreaming can help you solve problems, gain confidence and a new sense of empowerment and liberation in your life.

Here are some exercises to help you achieve lucid dreaming.

1.  **Reality Check.** During the day frequently ask yourself if you are dreaming. Do a reality check. You can even set your alarm to go off every hour as a reminder. With practice, you will automatically in time do the same in your sleep. Do a reality check every time something seems out of the ordinary or even when something seems frustrating. Do these often while awake and this habit you will carry with you in your sleep. You can do reality checks such as looking at your digital clock and seeing if the numbers stay the same. Read something and go back to see if it's the same for example. Poking yourself, you may find that in the dream your skin may be more

rubbery. Try pushing your finger through the palm of your hand. Lean against the wall. In a dream you will most likely fall through it.

2. **Keep a dream journal.** Keep it near your bed. You can also use a cassette recorder if you like. Write stuff down immediately upon awakening. Keeping a dream journal also allows you to recognize certain key elements in your dream. In dreams there are dream signs that we may not notice, such as bed outside by the ocean, or Angelina Jolie kissing you. In your journal on a separate page write down your dream signs. Taking Vitamin B6 or melatonin can help induce lucid dreams.

_____

_____

_____

_____

_____

_____

_____

_____

3. **Learn what the best time for your lucid dream.** By having a sleep schedule you arrange the sleep pattern to help cause lucid dreaming. Taking a nap a few hours after awakening in the morning, studies show that is the best time for lucid dreaming. Lucid dreaming happens during REM sleep, which is rapid eye movement. REM sleep is most dominant just before awakening. Dreams run in 60 minute cycles while sleeping. For dream recall its best to wake yourself up during one of these cycles.

4. **Dr. Stephen LaBerge has a technique called MILD technique, (mnemonic induction of lucid dreaming).** Set your alarm clock to wake you up in about 4 ½ hours. When you are awaken by the alarm clock, try to

remember the dream as much as possible. Just before you return to sleep imagine that you are in your previous dream and that you are aware that you are dreaming. Say an affirmation that you will be aware that you are dreaming. Convince yourself as you fall asleep.

5.  **WBTB (wake back to bed) technique.** That is to set the alarm for 5 hours after sleep. Then go back to sleep and after you wake up focus on lucidity.

6.  **Try WILD (wake initiated lucid dream) technique.** This means carry your awareness with you as you fall asleep. This will cause you to have lucid dreams right away. Meditate as you fall asleep. You can also listen to binaural beats to put you into Theta state, the state of dreaming.

7.  **Diamond Method.** Meditate. When you meditate visualize your life, awake and dream life as facets of a diamond. Realize that all these events are all happening at once and that it is your perceptions that arrange events in time linear. Therefore like each facet of a diamond is an individual experience all happening at the same time. The Dream Body experiences this as well.

8.  **In your dream journal look through your previous dreams and see if you recognize a pattern.** The pattern that you notice is called a dream sign. In the movie Inception, Leonardo Dicaprio's character dream sign was a spinning top. Every individual has their own dream sign. You may find a pattern such as your dream takes place at your house you grew up in as a child. Get in a habit of doing a dream check every time you recognize this dream sign.

9.  **Look ma, my hands.** For thirty minutes prior to sleep, look at the palm of your hands. And repeat to yourself "I will dream about (choose dream). Repeat phase as you look at your hands. After 30 minutes go to sleep. When you awake during the night, look at your hands, remind yourself that you will see your hands in next dream. With

practice your hands will just pop up in front of you in your dream. That will be a sign that you are dreaming.

**Tips**

- During lucid dreaming you can conquer fears. If you are afraid of spiders for example, in a dream you can see them as amusing as a way to conquer your fears of them.
- When you know that you are dreaming make sure you know it's a dream at all times. There are no social consequences because all the people in your dreams are imaginations. You cannot get hurt; any pain is just in your imagination. You have total control of everything that includes your actions, the actions of everyone, your environment and the laws of physics.
- Visualize something in your hand. Feel its weight shape and texture. You can even do this to create a weapon in your hand to defeat an enemy by changing your nightmare.
- You can teleport. Close your eyes and see the environment change before you as you open your eyes.
- To control specific things in your dream, practice them while you are awake. Example, turn light off and on slowly during the day, and while sleep try the same.
- Fly in your dreams. It is exhilarating. While walking bounce higher and higher with each step. Some people can fly naturally. You can even try to walk on walls and the ceiling. Try passing your hand through a solid object and feel the texture of the object pass through your hand.
- Don't worry about what may happen in a dream, for it is only a dream. Nothing there can hurt you.

Worrying if someone will attack you in the dream, most likely they will, so relax.

In lucid dreaming you can then master your dreams and wake up feeling good. This in return will cause good things to happen to you in your daily life. Some people naturally know that they are dreaming, but do nothing to master it. They just react to the dream. Illumination also called Enlightenment is also realizing that in waking life that all is a dream. The problem is when one decides not to take actions because they think everything is meaningless because all is just a dream. Being apathetic causes one to lose desire which then causes depression. This state is called the "dark night of the soul." In this state one feels alone because everything around them is just a dream and everything they felt that meant something to them loses their value. This feeling is due to lack of desire. When you lack desire, you are not in tune with the desire of the God Source within. When you desire something, it is your God within speaking. To not have desire is ignoring the God within. You may be aware that everything is a dream, but you are ignoring God within, when you are apathetic about everything. The All That Is wants you to grow. Desire is necessary for growth. The God source wants you to become the person necessary to have and do the things you want. You cannot have desire for something you cannot achieve. If you have desire for it, which means that, you can achieve it.

Without desire nothing would exist. Desire comes from the Source many calls God. The black hole attracts and accumulates electricity. Gravitation is the desire of electricity to integrate into the appearance of form. Once the electricity is accumulating in the black hole then what radiates outward is magnetism. Radiation is the desire of magnetism to disappearance of form. Magnetism is the reaction from electricity being accumulated. These opposites spiral around the black hole in opposite directions. These opposite forces are simultaneously taking place in all matter. Electricity is the inhalation and gathers power.

Magnetism is the exhalation that dissipates power bringing things to rest. Electricity and magnetism are not two different forces; they are different expressions of motion of the same force.
All this happens because of desire, desire from the One, the Consciousness that permeates all. Therefore since our true Self is the Source, that we are God, then it is natural to have desire. Desire is the motive power behind force and motion. Without desire there can be no motion or force. Desire is the cause of the apparent division of the father-mother (Positive-negative) substance of Consciousness into opposites. This division is due to the opposite desires of electricity and magnetism, expressed in the action' and reaction of the thinking process. From this other mothers and fathers are reproduced. As the spiraling of electricity and magnetism reproduces as it fractals, an atom is finally born (Figure 6. 10). This process keeps happening as other mothers and fathers are manifested until everything that exist manifest. This manifestation is continuously. There is no ending to the reproduction. Life and death is happening simultaneously. Life is expressed through electricity that is inhaled into the gravity center of Consciousness; death is expressed through magnetism that is exhaled from the gravity center of Consciousness. Everything is constantly being reproduced to give forms in the Universe. Desire causes the uniting of opposites into one which then continues on forever.

Sex and Desire are connected, for they are the same. Sex is of the sacral center and associated with creativity. The Third Eye is to command. The sex force which is desire is needed to command. Sex reproduces through union of opposites. Love causes union of opposites that have similarity. Desire is love. Love is God. God is Consciousness. Consciousness is Gravity.

Figure 6.10
The structure of the atom. All effects of motion are repeative. Size is purely relative. The heavens swarm with replicas of atoms of all the elements.

Every action has an equal and opposite reaction, which is Newton's third law of motion. This is how electricity and magnetism works. Within our little minds the same principle applies. When we focus on something in our minds, we then attract to us through our experiences what we focus on. Events and people appear in our lives that reflect what we are focusing on. Just like when we are dreaming in our sleep, all experiences are our creation. In waking life we draw events and other real people into our lives that reflect our mood. Since those people appear, we are also drawn into what they focus on. It is an unconscious agreement that is taking place between all the participants, everyone subconsciously fulfilling the roles to play in each of our lives.

If an individual has victim mentality he/she will subconsciously draw other people into their lives to confirm that they are a victim. Before they realize it, they are a victim to unsavory characters. For one to stop being a victim, they first have to change how they think. A way to begin changing your thoughts is to be proactive daily.

Lucid dreaming is the step to realizing that all is a dream. As I said earlier that psychic phenomena can be access through lucid dreaming, lucid dreaming can also be a doorway to astral projection. In the heart center, one realizes that the body is a machine, and here in the six spiral (Third Eye center) is where astral projection can easily take place.

In one myth, when Set and Horus were fighting for the throne after Osiris's death, Set gouged out Horus's left eye. The majority of the eye was restored by Hathor or Thoth (with the last portion possibly being supplied magically). When Horus's eye was recovered, he offered it to his father, Osiris, in hopes of restoring his life. Hence, the eye of Horus was often used to symbolize sacrifice, healing, restoration, and protection.

In this myth, the message is that by having the Third Eye open, one can also heal and restore life. This is the realm of what is also called Christ Consciousness. In this state you realize that everything that exist first exist in the Mind. All that exists first existed in the Mind of All That Is. The All That Is is what many call God. The life energy follows the mind. Just as the universe is manifested from the idea that came from the desire from Consciousness, that life energy also bends according to our will. Due to lack of self-awareness, our ability to control this energy is limited. The more aware we become of the true Self, the easier it is to control the life energy that gives life to all forms.

In the book The book of Coming Forth By Day (The Egyptian Book of the Dead), a term "Smai Tawi" is used. It means "Union of the two lands of Egypt. The two lands refer to the two main districts of the country (North and South). In ancient times, Egypt was divided into two sections. These were known as Lower and Upper Egypt. In Ancient Egyptian mystical philosophy, the land of Upper Egypt relates to Horus, who represents the Higher Self, and the land of Lower Egypt relates to Set, the lower self. So Smai Taui means "the union of the two lands" or the "Union of the lower self with the Higher Self.

The lower self is the base self that is uncontrolled without the Higher Self. When the lower self is uncontrolled it leads to ignorance and fear. The Higher self is related to transcendental consciousness (Horus). Therefore the union of Horus and Set is Yoga which means to yoke. It is about the union of duality. The three higher energy centers are in union with the three lower energy centers. With this union there is non-duality which leads to the One singular consciousness. In this state you have mastery of your experiences. Whatever you desire you can achieve. Sometimes what make the path hard are the conflicting emotional beliefs that we harbor. We intellectual believe everything that this book is saying, but emotional many of us do not. In many of our emotional beliefs we believe we are separate from each other and doubt if we are worthy to have our desires meant. Emotional beliefs will always win over our intellectual beliefs. Lucid dreaming is away to help change our emotional beliefs. Through direct experiences of mastering the dream we gain the self confidence that we carry with us when we are awake. This sense of empowerment allows us to manifest our dreams when we are awake. Experience itself is what changes our beliefs.

When it comes to commanding your dreams, hold in your mind's eye what it is that you want. Feel that you already accomplished it. Knowing this and taking actions your desires will manifest. If you desire having it, then you can achieve it.

Some people will argue and say, "Well that's not so, because I haven't acquired my desires," they would say. Well if a desire didn't manifest it is either because it was just a wish or fantasy, or if it was a desire then either you didn't stick with it and gave up, or you only pursued it in a half ass manner or you doubted yourself and didn't even attempt to take action. Those are the only reason why a desire didn't manifest.

The stronger the desire for something the faster and stronger it will manifest. As in the third law of motion, "every action has an equal reaction", that means the more you put out, the more that comes back. If you throw a basketball hard against the wall, the harder it will bounce back. Desire for something, acts just like the basketball. What bounces back will manifest in material form through events, situations and people.

There is no separateness and the more we realize that, the more we realize that everything we want is at arm's reach.

Consciousness is like an Ocean. That Ocean of Consciousness is God. If we scoop a cup of water from the ocean into a glass, does that mean the water in the glass is different? No it does not. We are the water in different glasses. For the water in the glass to say it's different than the Ocean is no different than when we say we are separate from God. Intuition is direct communion with God within you that permeates all existence.

The light of the body is the eye: therefore when thine eye is single, thy whole body also is full of light; but when thine eye is evil, thy body also is full of darkness. – Luke 11:34.
Here in the Christian bible this reference is talking about the Third Eye. The degree of clearness the Third Eye seeing reflects the whole body. When the Third Eye is open your body is full of Light. You see clearly and truly understand the Laws of Creation. You realize that you are not your experiences and that all is an extension of you and therefore you can control the world around you. You realize that by truly following the Laws of Creation is the most rational approach to living. You then Ascend as a Master.

On the other hand when your Eye is cloudy very little Light enters into you. The average person is very much like an old television with poor reception. The old television receives fuzzy reception. The average individual receives fuzzy reception from the God Source. Through meditation certain chemicals are released in the brain which opens the Third Eye and allows us to get clear reception like cable television. We then receive clearly the reception of the God Source to where we come to realize the God Source is our true Self. In this constant state of communion with the God within, this is what you call prayer without ceasing.

When the Eye is cloudy the reception is so poor that our whole view of everything is dark. In darkness we become ignorant to the All That Is. In this darkness we feel lost and indecisive and unconfident in the decisions we make during difficult situations. You feel that everything is separate and out of reach and spiritually lost as your true purpose is unclear. This uncertainty and fear creates fear of lost which sometimes manifest as greed and jealousy and other unpleasant emotions. The more cloudy the Eye, the more one walks in ignorance. The more one walks in ignorance the more fear and impulsive reactions one makes in life. Individuals in this state can be dangerous when they become so attach to power whether it's in the form of money or manipulation. They feel that they are worthless without power, so power becomes their addiction in order to feel like half a person.

When the energy centers are cloudy we walk in ignorance. The way we clear that Eye to let the Light clear all our energy centers is by having the Life Force flow to the brow entering the Astral Body that nourish and burns away the ignorance, allowing us to see.

When the wholeness of the Third Eye is achieved, there is no power that can withstand its force. This practice of affirming and asserting the true power that is within must go on daily so that it may have its full transformative effect on the mind. Positive affirmations and the study of the teachings should be a daily practice until the wholeness of the Eye is achieved. Even after that, it is something that must continue or the Eye will become cloudy again. There is no point where your work is finished. Once the Eye is clear for it to stay open, proper actions must always be taken.

Pleiadian Spirals of Light

# THE SEVENTH SPIRAL
## (Element *Thought*)

The Seventh spiral of the Crown Center is on the top of the head. It is the center of Understanding. It is associated with the element Thought. This Power Center is about Understanding. Here is a correspondent of the symbolism of this power center.

**Element:** Thought
**Function:** Understanding
**Glands:** Pituitary
**Unbalances:** Depression, alienation, boredom
**Color:** Violet
**Sephira:** Kether

This seventh spiral is about Understanding. This is the realm of Cosmic Consciousness. Here is about understanding about the true Self. Cosmic Consciousness is being aware that the universe exists as an interconnected network of consciousness where every conscious being is connected to each other.

There is only one Source. There is only one Universe. There is only one Light. That Light is the Universe, that Light is the All That Is, which many call God. The Universe and God are not separate. There is no created universe. Everything that exists always was. There is no beginning and no ending.

Man sees Creation as something that came into existence from something that didn't exist before. Man's view of the Creator is a separate being that created the physical universe that didn't exist before. Man sees that God created an imperfect physical universe and a supernatural spiritual one of perfection. The truth is that God cannot create anything imperfect and there is no supernatural. All is natural and the Source doesn't create anything lesser or greater than Itself. All is Light and Light is Life and there is only one Life. The substance of universal Consciousness is a living substance. Nothing is created; this is a creating universe, not a created one. The one Light has full awareness of Itself. God has full awareness of Himself/ Herself. As the Light manifest extensions of itself, the fractal lacks most of its awareness. The hydrogen atom which is the first atom manifested has all the original information of God within it, but has very little awareness of itself. This lack of awareness causes it to have the appearance of limitations. As each manifestation of atoms appears they gradually become more aware of itself. The keyboard on the piano vibration changes slightly than the one preceding it, it is the same with atoms, each one vibrates slightly different and the awareness of itself is slightly more than the one manifested preceding it. All the atoms are married to another atom except the atom of carbon. Carbon is neutral and has no marriage partner, like the Heart Center is neutral and has no partner. All the atoms are created inside a star. Once they are all created the star implodes and explodes as a super nova. The dust and gases from the former star lumps together to become a new sun with planets revolving around it which becomes a solar system. A planet that has the right temperature and has water something wonderful happens. When water mixes with carbon and other minerals two chemical compounds called DNA and RNA is formed. From both comes all that we perceive as life. This RNA and DNA have more self-awareness than the minerals that gave birth to it. It all depends on how sugar molecule and phosphate molecule which forms a nucleotide that determine what DNA strands are formed. Each life that manifest is more aware than the previous. Plants are more aware than minerals. Crustaceans and insects are more self-aware than the fish of the sea. Birds are more self-aware than reptiles. Mammals are more self-aware than birds. Primates are more self-aware than all the previous animals. Even though primates such as lemurs, monkeys and apes are the most self-aware preceding us, their level of self-awareness is limited. What is interesting is that the great apes have 24 chromosomes and humans have 23. It is that one less chromosome that makes us different. When it comes to humans the level of self-awareness potential is unlimited. Many of us don't seem to be that much more advance than the monkeys, but our potential of self-awareness is unlimited. When compared to the Kabbalistic Tree of Life (Figure 7.1) we fit in the category of Kether. The properties of Kether are limitless light.

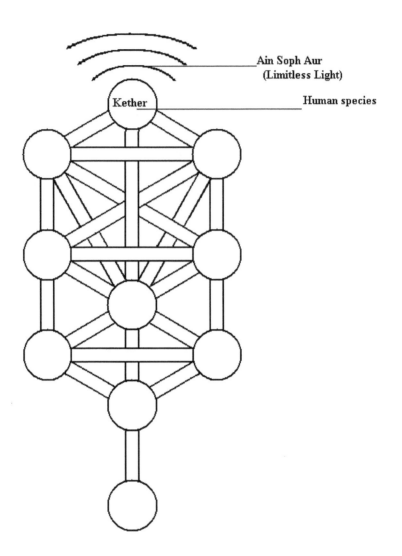

Figure 7.1
Human species position on the Tree of Life
On the sephira Kether on the Tree of Life, is in Malkuth and Malkuth is a reflection of Kether like the root center is a reflection of the crown center. The root is married to the crown.

In the first spiral of the root center when strong, there is no self-judgment. Self-judgment cannot exist if you realize that you are not separate from anything else. When you realize that you are not what you experience, then you are beyond self-judgment and self-esteem. You have no need to prove anything to anyone. No need to flaunt your ego. When the root and crown is strong, you are the One. There is no duality and you are totally secured as you have immense gratitude of universal love toward yourself and others. Life is so grateful in this state of infinite awareness.

That which is called God is holographic. All act when God act, but guess what God doesn't act, and neither do you. Motion is an illusion caused by reproduction and disintegration of form. This inhalation and exhalation of force is a continuous process that takes place. The creating universe appears from the One and disappears into the One. (Figure 7.2) Everything that comes from God is returned to God. The ouroboros (Figure 7.3) which is the symbol of the dragon or serpent eating its own tail shows this. All that comes from the Source is returned to the Source, this recycle is a continuous process.

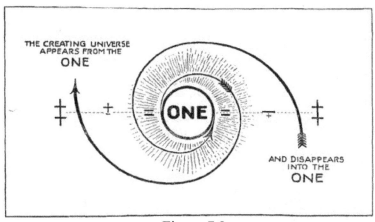

Figure 7.2
All comes from the One and disappears into the One.

Figure 7.3
Serpent eating its own tail representing
the complete circle.

The seventh spiral is Universal Consciousness. Now the question is what consciousness is? Consciousness is the universe. It is all that is, and ever will be. Consciousness is a substance, a material substance. The substance of Consciousness is the foundation of creation. It is the seed of the universe. In the seed of the universe is the whole of the universe. The substance of universal Consciousness has no beginning, no ending and no bounds. It is all intelligent, all-powerful and permeates everywhere and is a living force.

As a thinking substance desire creates opposing forces that give the appearance of form. It is the opposing forces within it that cause it to be thinking. All the qualities of matter such as texture, temperature does not exist in Consciousness, but the opposing forces from thinking give it appearances of those qualities of matter. Matter itself has no existence accept in the appearance of existence. The cause of appearance of change is the change of state, but in truth nothing changes. Change of state is not a character of substance; it is the illusion of motion which creates the illusion of dimension. When you look at a television screen the images appear to have dimension and movement. Light waves come through the screen and the pixels (Figure 7.4) which are tiny squares light up in different colors to give the appearance of images, these colors change 30th of a second giving the appearance of movement.

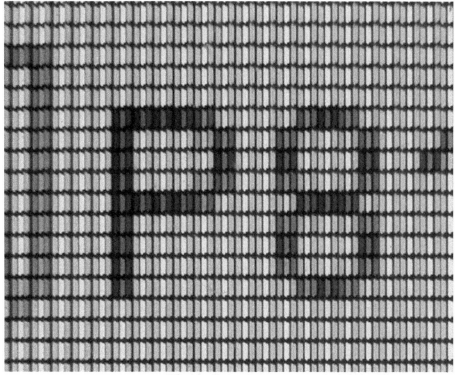

Figure 7.4
Pixel squares change color frequency 30th of second giving the illusion of movement.

The material substance of Consciousness is an all permeating spirit which is indestructible, unchangeable and inseparable which gives the appearances of separation of different material objects. We are very much like the pixels on a television and computer screen. As in the diagram of the pixels it is the color frequency within each pixel square that lights up that give the appearance of dimension. The images on the screen appear to be separate from each other, but the whole screen is filled with pixels. There is no space between the images, for the screen is filled with pixels. Within the universe there is no empty space. Consciousness that pervades all is filled with energy. Without the illusion of separation, there would be no space. Without events there would be no time. Time only exist in the mind which measures a duration of events.

All is Light, Consciousness is Light. Man is trying to figure out what the force is that holds things together. They have trouble understanding this force because they only view one side of the force. Because they only view the force one sided, they say it's very weak, but also seems strong when it comes to large heavenly bodies. Man named this unknown force as gravity. Newton realized that gravity pulls things downward toward heavenly bodies, such as the earth. What many fail to see is that gravity does much more than that. It pulls similar vibrations together. The water vapors are pulled upward by gravity towards other gaseous substances. Gravity is Consciousness and in the center of every spiral is a blackhole. Blackholes do not just exist in space, they exist everywhere. Through the thinking process of Consciousness (Gravity) electricity (male) which is predominately positive polarity gravitates inward into the blackhole and magnetism (female) which is predominately negative polarity radiates outward from the blackhole. This curved motion spirals in opposite directions. From this unfolding of these forces from the centering seed of Consciousness eventually manifest the atom. Electricity and magnetism spirals around a centering blackhole. Even the electricity that travels in a wire is spiraling around a centering blackhole.

Frequency is repetition of pulsations. Pulsations are reproduction of the opposing forces. How often the pulsations are determines the speed and frequency of manifested forces. Examine a strobe light that pulses. The two opposing forces is the light radiating out from the bulb, and the opposing force is the light disappearing. The repetition of the light appearing and disappearing gives the strobe light the effect of the pulsating bulb. The speed of the pulsation determines the frequency. Everything has its own unique pattern of pulsations. Electricity and magnetism does the same. Once it reaches a certain frequency an atom is born. In actuality electricity and magnetism are not different forces. They are the same moving in different directions giving the appearance of separate forces. Magnetism is just the reaction from the action of electricity. When you throw a basketball at a wall, the ball bouncing back is the reaction from the action of the ball being thrown. The faster you bounce the ball off the wall, the faster the frequency. This is the same with electricity and magnetism. The blackhole takes in energy in the form of electricity and it bounces out as magnetism like the ball bouncing off the wall. Even if you change the pattern and speed of how you bounce the basketball off the wall, nothing has changed. The ball is still the same ball being bounced, the only thing different is the pace you choose to bounce the ball. If you bounce the ball 10 times within 10 seconds that frequency is 10 bounces /10 seconds. If you bounce the ball 20 times within 10 seconds, now the frequency of the bounce has changed to 20 bounces/10 seconds. When the blackhole absorbs energy in the form of electricity and bounces out magnetism, it is still the same energy, and it's the pattern of repetition that determines what substance it appears.

The universe is much like the music keys on the piano. Each key note has a slightly different frequency then the previous note. The speed of pulsation determines by the length of the piano string. If all the piano strings have equal tension, the longer strings will have a lower tone. That means the pulsation or vibration is slower. It has a lower frequency. On a piano our ears are able to pick up the slight differences of frequency on each key prior to the previous. When it comes to visible light for example, our ears cannot hear that the color red has a lower frequency than the other colors (Figure 7.5) after it. Instead our eyes pick up the difference in the appearance of different colors, each color slightly different than the previous.

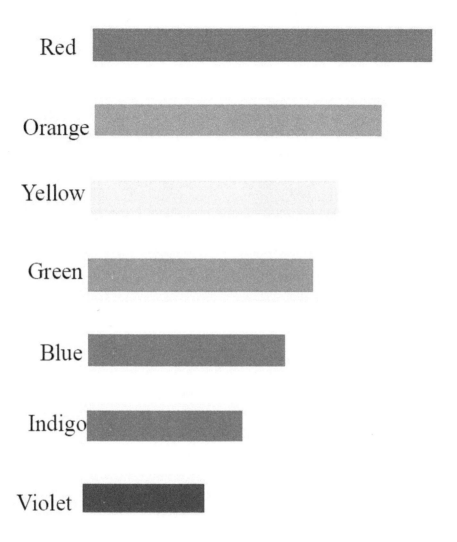

Figure 7.5
The longer the wavelength, the lower the frequency of the wavelength. Red has the lowest. If it was a piano string I's tone would be the lowest of the color spectrum.

Each atom that manifest have a slightly different vibration than the atom before it. This is much like the piano key minor C is slightly different in tone as major C that precedes it. Major D is slightly different in frequency tone than minor C that precedes it. This is a process that gradually happens until all the atoms exist. When certain atoms join together to form molecules, it is like different notes on the piano playing to create music. Each molecule is like a music piece. Even though each piano key is no different than each other except in the length of piano wire, just by playing certain notes together, you get the appearance of multiple music pieces. In truth the different vibrations of energy give the appearance of different sounds, but the notes put together in a certain arrangement gives the appearance of music.

Let's take the example of the basketball again. If you were able to bounce the ball a 100 times per second, it will sound like a steady sound at a certain tone. If you took that same ball and bounce it 200 times, it will still have a steady sound, but the pitch would be higher. Our senses perceive this as two separate sounds, but it is still the basketball bouncing off the wall. Not only do we do this with our hearing, all our senses do the same thing, fool us into perceiving separate and different smells, textures and colors when it is the same continuous energy that is spiraling into the blackhole and spiraling back out. The only difference is the pace of repetition of energy drawn and exhaled out the blackhole.

Let's say hypothetically if you bounced the ball 430 trillion times, the pitch will be too high to even hear a sound, but instead your eyes will see the color red. Of course this is not humanly possible, but it is just an example to show how our different senses receive different appearances of the same thing.

Everything is Light. Light is the living substance of Consciousness in action. Spirit is light, matter is light. Spirit and matter are the same substance; the substance of Universal Consciousness is a living substance. Energy is a living substance, and there is only One energy that exist everywhere, it cannot be divided. A hertz is a cycle per second. In the basketball example, a cycle would be the ball bouncing off the wall one time. For every action there is an equal reaction. Every action is male (positive) polarity. Every reaction is female (negative) polarity. The speed of repetition of a cycle is what gives appearances of form to all things we perceive. When the cycle of pulses of energy is 430 trillion pulses in a second, which is 430 trillion hertz, you will perceive the color red. As the number of pulses increase, you will see the color orange and all the way up to violet which is 750 trillion hertz. Radio waves are less than 3 billion hertz.

Human ears can detect frequency from 25 to 18,500 hertz. When we talk our voices are between 800 to 5000 hertz. The telephone is around 3000 hertz so that we can still understand someone speaking. 4000 hertz is the most irritating frequency; this is the frequency of fingernails screeching the chalk board. The lowest C note on the piano is 32 hertz, whereas the highest note on the piano is 4096 hertz.

The five sensory organs interpret the frequencies as color, odors, taste, sound, and texture. What one organ picks up sometimes the other organs do not. We do not hear colors or smell them. If all our senses picked up everything, it would be overwhelming.

**Life:** There is One life. Life is the pulsating electromagnetic repetitive cycles of thinking Consciousness. Life is the property of all matter, all matter is life. What is breathing? Breathing is pulsation and everything pulsates. Vibration is pulsation. Strike a guitar string and it pulsates. This rapid pulsation is vibration. Oscillating waves are spirals perceived from a different angle. Observe the toy called slinky. Look at the slinky face on it is a spiral of metal wire. Look at it sideways and stretch it, it will look like waves. (Figure 7.6)

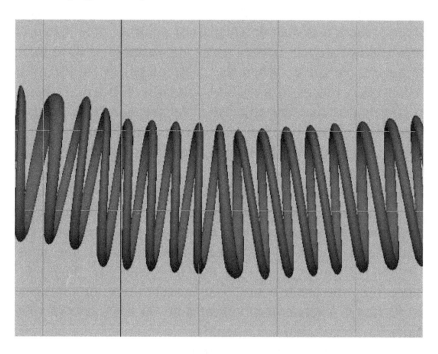

Figure 7.6
Slinky coil resembling a wave

Most of mankind here on planet earth view life as separate from matter and that life only begins in organic forms. They view non organic material as lifeless. All things are alive, all things are pulsating. Our senses are limited so we only perceive organic forms as living. Only life comes from life, therefore all living things came from life. Life cannot come from non-life, therefore energy itself is alive. Life has no beginning and no ending; it always was and is eternal. Some will say death is natural and all things die. Death is a state of entropy; it is the disappearance of form. All form that disappears is reproduced, therefore nothing really dies, and it just changes its state.

Consciousness, matter, light and energy are one and are eternal. There is no true death, for reproduction and disintegration are constant cycles of motion, which is an effect.

The cause of all motion is the action of thinking of the One universal living Energy, which man calls God, Consciousness, or other names, all of which stand for the idea, of a deity. Thinking is a process, an evolutionary pattern of cycles. Pattern comes from the word pater which means father. The father gives the seed which is the pattern which causes a reaction of form. Mother comes the word mater, as well as the word matter. For something to matter it must first materialize, be mothered. That which radiates is mothered. All that radiates out from the center of the One is matter (mother). Throwing the basketball is the father. The ball bouncing back is the mother. The basketball that bounces back moves in the opposite direction. The magnetism that bounces back out from the blackhole curves in the opposite direction. All motion of thinking Consciousness is born in the maximum high speed of the universal constant of energy. The greater the generation of energy the greater the temperature and the greater the radiation and the finer matter appear. The lesser the generation of energy the lesser the temperature and the lesser the radiation and the coarser matter appears. Coarse matter is frozen light, which appear as form. That which appears as solid objects is just frozen light. The reason why two appearances of frozen light don't pass through each other is because when two similar electromagnetic poles are in contact they repel each other like two magnets that repel each other when faced the directions of the same pole. The similar electromagnetic field acts as a force field that gives the appearance of solidity and the sense of feeling texture by touch. When frozen light temperature rises it changes form giving the appearance of death.

We observe and see material substances such as iron rust and organic components break down to decay. Those things have reached its full potential of the limited self-awareness therefore it is time for those things to disappear in the form of decay to eventually come back again. Other animals beside man have limited self-awareness, a dog for example ages a lot faster than humans. There is no reason for a dog to live pass 14 to 20 years. A dog has reached his full potential within that time frame. Within 14 years a dog has aged 82 years of age. Since a dog has reached its full potential within that time frame, the only thing left is for the dog to transition to the next stage which is death. Humans on the other hand have an unlimited potential of self-awareness, therefore it is not unnatural to extend the life of human beings. No matter how long a human being lives he will never reach his/her full potential. If one's potential of self-awareness is unlimited, one can never reach that which has no boundaries. One can live billions of years and one still have potential for growth. One is not stuck in an unnatural unchanging immortal state, in appearance they may not look much different, but one is not the same. Are you the same person you were when you was 3 years of age? No you are not, you have those memories, but you do not even feel like you are that same person. You have grown in wisdom. Your views of life have changed, and you literally have a completely different body. The cells that made up your flesh years ago have been completely replaced.

Genius is a bridge between man and God within. This potential of genius is within everyone. It comes from the divine and nowhere else. Einstein received his revelation through meditation. Meditation is a way of communion with the All That Is.

What makes us different that other species is that since other species have a limited self-awareness they do not have to exercise will to become more aware by being better than we was the day before. Other species such as plants and other animals just rely on instinct. Just by relying on instinct they are in harmony with the laws of balnce.

As human beings since we have the unlimited potential of self-awareness we must frequently feed our self with knowledge that reveals our unlimited potential. When we do not feed for a while we experience growing pains. Growing pains are signals like physical hunger pains. Growing pains are known to be emotional difficulties during adolescent. Here since growth is a nonstop process, I will use the term growing pains for emotional difficulties in general. In life when we go a period without eating we get hungry. We then eat something which satisfies our hunger. Eventually we get hungry again and have to eat. The hunger pains are signals telling our body that we need to eat.

Since other species have a limit of self-awareness they do not have to feed themselves with knowledge to become more self-aware, they are already at their full potential, therefore functioning on instincts is enough.

When we are not feeding ourselves spiritually daily we get growing pains where we experience emotional difficulties. The longer we wait to do anything about it, the more painful the hunger grows. When we are spiritually starving, we become desperate and start making very impulsive choices. It is those reactive behaviors that cause disharmony in ours and other people's lives. The desperate become so self-centered that they do anything to get what they desperately seek to fill in the pit inside themselves that they don't care or even realize how their behavior is hurting others. An individual has the same degree of respect for others as they have for themselves. If one doesn't respect themselves they won't respect others or their things.

When this seventh spiral center is weak one will feel no connection to the divine. They will feel lost and alone. One may even feel that God has abandoned them and unworthy of spiritual help.

To make a comparison to physical food, if you go to long where you are starving, you get desperate. Now if you eat small frequent meals during the day, you won't have to experience hunger pains. This also applies to spiritual food. If you are being proactive daily to make yourself a better you than the previous day, then you will not experience emotional difficulties.

There is no separate force of evil. That which is perceived as evil is imbalance. When we are not in harmony with the Laws of Nature by being proactive daily, we then feel discomfort. We are not at ease, we are dis-eased. All the disharmony is caused by not being in balance with the Laws of Creation. This disharmony causes desperation. Desperation is fear that manifest as greed, self-centeredness, hate, and all the other emotions that creates behavior that causes disharmony in the world.

When we are in harmony with the Laws of Creation by being proactive daily, we see more clearly of the Oneness that exists. We realize that nothing of itself is alone and that all created things are united. This is the law of all the substance of Universal Consciousness. This is the law of love, the law of Oneness of the universe. The Oneness of the universe is simple One spiritual substance of Consciousness. The One substance of Consciousness is a living thinking Being of which all things are an extension of which is all united. Light is what makes of the One substance a living substance. Light are the life principle of Consciousness and the creating force of the universe. Light is all there is, all is Light. Realizing this, you do not feel alone, and you realize that you are not just a little mind in a huge universe.

Tapping into this great awareness of the One causes us to be in total communion with it, where it comes to us as information. Information is the perceived input of order that make up one's system. As a vehicle of consciousness it is natural to want to share the information. This information is expressed at a genius level. Meditation is like defragmenting your hard drive allowing more room for information without crashing your system with overload.

**Meditation and astral projection:** Mediation can open doors and expand the crown center. Meditation is the most important function of human development in the process of human growth. Many genius have practice mediation without fully aware of what it is. They call it introspection as they come up with ideas. These ideas are information coming from the Universal Soul. When you meditate you can accomplish anything you so desire. You can heal the body, master anything in your life, and become anything that you want. When you meditate you are in communion with the Universal Consciousness.

When you realize that your mind and Universal Consciousness are the same, you realize that you are Consciousness that is the glue of the universe. You then realize that you are God and are aware of the constant presence in every moment. Working knowingly with God, you are the co-creator with the divine. As co-creator with the divine you have the power to weave the web that controls the universe. By following your thoughts with actions, is expressing your eternal Self in the visible universe of matter.

Whatever you ask for, ask with your heart's desire, not with words. Each time you meditate you become more and more in communion with the Universal Consciousness which many call God. As you do, you receive more and more information from the divine Source. Your reception becomes clear like 3 D cable television. Many times we make the error of asking things with our senses instead of with our soul. When we rely on our physical senses they can distract you by creating doubt in yourself because it appears on the surface that nothing is happening. Our physical senses only see a certain percentage of what's going on and sometimes it blinds us. Therefore go beyond the physical senses and know in your heart it will manifest. You will always get what you ask God for. When we don't it is because we ask our senses and not God. Write your desire into your heart beat. When you do write your desire into your heart then you are asking God. When your desire in your heart is there your intuition is open for guidance that will lead you to take the proper actions to achieve your desire. Without this guidance you may not achieve what you want. If you do, it may take a lot longer.

Imagine your idea in the form of a concept; continue to visualize your desire until you see it clearly before you act upon it. Do not waist time experimenting. Wait until the image is clear with full intent. If you act on your desire in the physical world while it's in the embryotic state, it will not be mature. Whatever your desire is, whether it's an invention or a symphony, take it to God for a spiritual form. Examples, if it's a symphony hear the whole symphony in the silence of your soul first. If it's a sale, have it fully in your mind's eye what it is before you approach your clients. Don't let your ego senses get in the way, physical emotions can cloud your inspiration. Imagine before giving objective form and while calm you realize your desire will manifest. A master piece must have your soul extended to your product. If not it will not inspire others. If no love is extended to it, it is already dead.

Meditation can also be used for astral projection. Astral project is when the soul, human consciousness can leave the body. When the astral body leaves the body, there is many benefits. The astral body can venture out and explore many ways to improve itself which means once return to the physical body can improve all aspects of your well-being.

During astral projection you are able to see, feel and experience things most other people can barely even imagine. In doing so your consciousness will be raised, your negative energy will be at a minimum, and you will become aware of something far greater than your base self.

You will feel a sense of calm and self-acceptance wash over you. The fear of death and uncertainty will no longer affect you. You become liberated.

While astral projecting, you can tap into the Akashic Records– a universal source of infinite wisdom. This gives you a strong psychic ability that helps you retrieve hidden information, make important decisions and come up with solutions to certain challenges.

Astral projection opens up a whole new sense of psychic awareness you never knew you had. The benefits of this will enhance your health, career, finances and relationships. Astral projection can also increase your energetic vibration. When your vibrations increase, you will experience a deep sense of calm, a constant positive state of mind and a natural magnetism for people and possessions with similarly high vibrations, where you'll be able to create your ideal reality on autopilot, without the usual willpower struggles.

The reason why many people fail when applying the Law of Attraction, is because they are not in the right emotional state. They struggle with their will against the emotional beliefs for their new intellectual beliefs. Astral projection can solve this problem by opening your eyes to your limitless potential, and enhancing your self-awareness, spiritual connection by changing your belief system. By having your emotional and intellectual beliefs in harmony with each other, you can then with the power of intention to manifest the outcomes, things and people you want in your life.

When you enter into your meditation state, think deep down inside of your subconscious and create a visual image of your astral self. You can imagine your astral body into whatever shape you feel the most comfortable with. In the deep meditative state, imagine yourself raising your astral arm; this is a step toward astral projection.

Earlier I mentioned my initiated astral projection by a female entity, another time I partially astral projected on my own. The eve after Christmas the year 2005 I partially lifted out of my body and I had seen that I had wings and fell back into my body. This was the image of my astral self during that time. Your astral self can be in any shape.

While totally calm see yourself rise out of your body. It helps to have a destination. With practice you will succeed.

Meditation is the journey towards the Self. We must transcend body and mind. The more we meditate the more our Self-knowledge expands. The more we meditate the more we reach God-awareness. When we reach this awareness of our true Self which is God then we gain more knowledge of the inner workings of the universe.

There are different meditation exercises. Some meditations are design to help one escape and ignore reality. These meditations are not beneficial. Imagining white light burning away negativity and going on through life believing that negativity is gone, isn't enough. Being aware of your issues and doing the work necessary to heal is what is needed. To heal, one must first be aware. You are not aware when you imagine all your problems burnt away from the white light. Meditation exercises should be done to make you more aware of yourself and your environment.

First sit comfortable anywhere. You must be comfortable with your back strait. Make sure your clothes are loose enough to be comfortable. Make sure the room temperature is comfortable for you. It is best to meditate on a slight empty stomach, for you don't want hunger pains to distract you either. Sit in chair you can choose to have legs cross or not. However you choose to sit, the back must be strait so that the flow of energy in the vortexes will flow freely. Close your eyes. Stop all inner dialogue. In your mind, be silent and relax. Take three slow deep breaths and relax even more. When our legs are crossed with clasp fingers, the energy circle is formed and gives more stability. Eyes are suggested to be closed. There are some types of meditations that are open eyed meditation. You can follow the rhythm of your breath, gaze at a candle flame or just observe your thoughts going by without judging them. Realizing that you are not your thoughts help tune you into the Oneness.

With all of these practices, it takes repetition of working on these practices, in due time you will become the mastery of the universe.

# LOVE AS THE INTEGRATOR

Love is the integrator. Love is the glue that binds all the energy centers. All the three lower Power Centers are married to the three higher Power Centers, they support each other. All of the Power Centers are both male and female polarity, but more dominate in one. The three lower ones have to do with more action, so I would say they are dominantly male. The Heart Power Center is the neuter that links the three bottom Power Centers with the three top Power Centers. In the first spiral survival depends on standing on your own two feet. When you have self-acceptance you are beyond judgment as you always feel loved and wanted by your friends. This self-acceptance comes from recognizing the God within. Actions are taking to take care of your physical body and dispelling automatic irrational thoughts.

This Power Center is married to the crown seventh spiral. Being grounded is not relying on crutches where you feel that you have to rely on something outside oneself to function. Being grounded is when you can stand on your own feet because you realize that you are that Universal Consciousness that is the All That Is. You realize that all that exists is the one Light that permeates existence.

In the second Power Center is where you feel worthy to have love. Intimacy comes from trust that you will not be hurt. When you learn to nurture yourself and have a healthy outlook about yourself then you will chose healthy relationships and see relationships as wonderful. Those who have intimacy problems associate intimacy with pain.

Tantra sees that all matter is energy and all energy is a manifestation of Consciousness. In the second spiral we can bond with the All That Is through Tantra. The second spiral is married to the sixth spiral which is about seeing through the Eye of God.

Pleiadian Spirals of Light

In the second spiral when you are balanced you realize there is no ownership, because no one can truly own anything when all is an extension of the Source who you are part of. Seeing through the Third Eye on the sixth spiral you take the creative energies from the second spiral to command what you want on the material plane. Command is the mother reaction from the active creative energies from the second spiral. On the sixth spiral level you create the future by commanding it. At this level the command is almost on autopilot.

On the third spiral it is about personal power through the use of will. The will to use to get your needs met. On this level when balanced, you are assertive in your actions. You put trivial immediate pleasures to the side to go for long term goals. You stand up for yourself and don't let others walk on you to avoid conflict. Here you exercise to get your needs met and this spiral is married to the fifth spiral where the outcome of personal power is speaking your voice. On the fifth spiral you speak with body language, telepathy and your voice to work the magic of getting your needs met. This combination is true personal power.

The Fourth spiral is the neutral center. It has the male and female in balance and is not married to any of the centers. It is the Power Center that unites all the centers together. The other centers cannot work without the Light of love. To stand on your own two feet in the first spiral requires self-acceptance which is love. To have healthy sexual relationships in the second spiral one must have self-love. Love is necessary to have to be able to see that intimacy is good instead of associated with pain. To have personal power and the will to exercise to get your needs requires love and respect for yourself to know that you are important and deserve to get your needs met, therefore you speak and express yourself through your fifth center. Love is what is needed to see through the Eye of God, for God is love, and love is necessary to see life through a bird's eye view. Love is necessary for the seventh spiral for here you realize that all that exists is love. You realize that everything is One and that Oneness is Love.

# POWER CENTER TEST

Here is a test that you can take to see what energy centers are strong or weak.

Answer each question to best of your ability

S = Strong Agree
A = Agree
F = Fairly
D = Disagree
SD = Strongly Disagree

Score zero point for S, one point for A, two points for F, three points for D and four points for SD. Add up the points for each Spiral.

## First Spiral (grounding, Survival)

|  | Answer | Score |
|---|---|---|
| I feel like I have a hard time manifesting what I want. | S A F D SD | |
| I worry about making wrong choices and going the wrong way. | S A F D SD | |
| I am confused about my purpose in life and having confidence | S A F D SD | |
| | **Total:** | |

## Second Spiral (Sexuality, Creativity)

|  | Answer | Score |
|---|---|---|

| I feel like I'm not worthy to be here. | S A F D SD |
| I feel like my sex life sucks | S A F D SD |
| It is hard to enjoy spending alone time. | S A F D SD |

**Total:**

## Third Spiral (Personal Power, Will)

Answer Score

| I often feel powerless to change my circumstances. | S A F D SD |
| I tend to give my power to others and put myself second. | S A F D SD |
| It seems bad things always happen to me | S A F D SD |

**Total:**

## Fourth Spiral (Love, Relationships)

Answer Score

| I don't feel worthy of love. | S A F D SD |
| I have a hard time expressing forgiveness. | S A F D SD |
| I have trouble trusting others. | S A F D SD |

**Total:**

# Fifth Spiral (Communication, Creativity)

**Answer  Score**

I have a hard time saying what I think and feel.  S A F D SD
I tend to say what I think others want to hear.   S A F D SD
I feel like other people don't hear me, and a hard
time expressing my ideas clearly.            S A F D SD

**Total:**

# Sixth Spiral (Intuition, Seeing)

**Answer  Score**

I have a hard time seeing my life any differently
 that it currently is, I feel like things will never
change.                                S A F D SD

I have a hard time feeling like I get any spiritual
answers and guidance.                  S A F D SD

I get headaches frequently.            S A F D SD

**Total:**

## Seventh Spiral (Awareness, Wisdom)

**Answer   Score**

I feel lost and would like more guidance on
getting on my spiritual path.                    S A F D SD
I feel unworthy of spiritual assistance;
I have a hard time feeling like I receive
 inspiration.                                     S A F D SD

I feel like I God has abandoned me, and
that my prayers and meditations are not
acknowledged .                                    S A F D SD

**Total:**

Add the score together for each part. Scores from 9-13 indicates that your vortexes are strong. 0-3 indicates that they are very weak and 6-8 is average. Look at what is weak and strong. Is your score higher in the lower or higher centers? Most important is does the results agree with you.

Sometimes when we are strong in a center and weak in its partner. Example you may have a high score in the crown energy center but weak in the root energy center. In this case you may have awareness and receive heighten ideas, but because the root center is weak, it is not reaching its partner at the crown and the results is that you barely finish projects and struggle to make the changes in your life even though you have the knowledge of what to do. If your second spiral center is weak then the flow will not meet with the cosmic flow from the crown. The five major energy centers above will be hindered. To fix this, one would need to work on the sex area to allow the sexual energy to reach the rest of the body. Each center is a combination of earth and cosmic energy that needs to come to balance. When we are blocked in any of these areas, we then put more emphasis on another energy center. For example, someone who is blocked in the heart center may put more emphasis in the sexual area. We tend to do this to compensate for what is lacking. Someone who is weak in the crown energy center may put more emphasis in the root energy center where they become attach to the security that they do have in that area.

Our relationships and what we are attracted too, has a lot to do with our energy centers. When we are attracted to an art piece, whether its music or a painting, it is because our energy center has a similarity to the artist that created it. When we don't like a music piece or any other art work, it is because there is a conflict with our energy centers and the artist that create the piece of art.

This also applies to relationships. We are attracted subconsciously too similar as well as what we lack and admire in the other. When we lack a trait in us that we wish we had, we then are attracted to others who have those qualities. In this case is how opposites attract.

# LILITH SPEAKS

I am the Seer of Desire, I am Lilith. When it comes to relationships get rid of negative self-disillusion. Do not settle. I represent power and individuality. Women do not retaliate in emotional realms by shutting down your sexuality. This is the time to rise up and realize your equality among the men.

We all have a soul mate; part of the work here is for you to rediscover each other. Bad dates, unhealthy relationships temp one to give up. Keep your eyes on the prize and stop settling. To think love is not high on the priority and that your career is more important, is a lie.

You cannot do real work without your soul mate, no matter how successful you appear. Go and find your matching half, don't give up by throwing in the tile.

If you are already in relationship, are you staying because of fear? Out of loneliness? Are you settling because you don't think anything can be different? Do not settle because you are looking for someone to save you from yourself. You have to heal yourself before you find your soulmate. He/she could be at arm's reach, even right in front of you, and you must be whole (healed) to find them. Sometimes you both need to grow before you can be together, and while you wait, it may seem hopeless, but endure as you know you will when you are both ready. When you are ready, they will be ready too, because you both are linked.

Stand and get what is entitled to you. The reason why you haven't is because you don't expect true happiness. Finding your soul mate is part of your destiny. Don't fall into the trap of thinking that it doesn't apply to you, or you will give up on desire. See and know it's coming to you and it will. If you say it won't, it will slip past you. You must be open to the Light, God will place people in your life at the right time as soon as you are ready. As a Seer of Desire I command desire at will, and that which is desire shall be brought forth. Therefore I say to you, what you desire shall be brought through as well.

I am the daughter of Fortitude and ravished every hour from my youth. For behold, I am Understanding, and science dwelleth in me. Science and occult can be scientifically explained. Science and spirituality complement each other. Science and religion has tried to separate from each other, the time now is when the bridge between the two shall meet. My garments are from the beginning, and my dwelling place is in myself. The Lion knoweth not where I walk; neither do the beasts of the field understand me. I am deflowered, yet a virgin; I sanctify and am not sanctified. Happy is he that embraceth me: for in the night season I am sweet, and in the day full of pleasure. My company is a harmony of many symbols, and my lips sweeter than health itself. I am Lilith the emissary of the hidden Light. The light in your life may be hidden, but it is there.

When you plant a seed in ground, do you see the fruit right away? All things that bear fruit stay hidden for a time. If you allow time for the concealment of hidden, with patience, good things will happen. Hurry and you will have nothing but a dormant seed with nothing sprouting. Your patience will be tested while the fruit is hidden. For I am an Emissary of the Hidden light, the understanding, my job and the Emissaries of the Hidden Light are to sometimes cause resistance so that in order for you all to grow. One must bear the darkness before one can see the light. Your patience and ego will be tested, endure and realize the light will be revealed.

All great work requires an incubation state. An embryo inside an egg is in the incubation state. This is the time that you must be patience. It may appear that there is no light at the end of the tunnel, so to speak. The light that is hidden will be revealed in time. You are capable of so much more than you think you are. I am the Seer of Desire and that what you desire, must wait for. Patience. If you lack the desire to wait and see the Light then nothing will happen. Concealment. Silence is golden. Your seed can grow when you are not boasting about what you are doing.

To pass the test you must learn to overcome the thoughts such as patience will get me nowhere, I have to have it now, why no one realize how good I am. These are the automatic thoughts that will get in your way. It takes nine months for a child to be born from a womb. The pressure of the embryotic sack was necessary. The pressure of the eggshell of an egg is a necessary incubation process. The revelation is the birth from the concealment. This is the revelation of the hidden light.

Throughout history because of man's fear of the unknown, especially when it comes to sex, have demonized me and my children as agents of evil. Due to the male dominated chauvinistic culture of the Hebrews, strong independent women were seen as villains. In the Hebrew mythology I am seen as the mother of all demons because I refuse to bow down to Adam. Salome Antipas was seen as a villain responsible for the beheading of John the Baptist, just because she was a teenage girl who had a crush on John the Baptist and adored what he taught. Men tried to repress sex and when in the presence of a seductress woman, she was seen as evil. Due to this sexual repression from taboos, myths about me seducing men in their dreams came about. Men felt guilty and embarrassed when they woke up in the middle of the night with semen soaked in their pants. This repression is responsible for child molestation, sexual harassment, pornography and sexual addiction. These attachments are due to lack of fulfillment. I have no problem supporting the pornography industry, as long as it displays consenting adults. It is the sexual taboos men create are the only reason why it sells.

As Chohan of the Emissaries of the Hidden Light we have tested man so that they can grow. Some passed, but unfortunately some failed. Those who do not understand our ways did perceive us as demons. We are not here to create discord in the name of hate. We are here because we love the human race as we love all beings. We are here to strengthen you all. Know this. Understand this.

I AM LILITH, EMISSARY OF THE HIDDEN LIGHT

# CONCLUSION

Here we are at the end of this book, but our work is just the beginning. We have gradually been moving into the New Age of Aquarius which is the realm of knowledge. For the longest time people have been going by belief systems without questioning anything. Now we are heading to the age where we choose to test without believing and knowing by the results. As we move into this age we will start to realize that we are all the Sons and Daughters of God as we come to realize that God is within.

December 21, 2012 mass sightings all over the globe have made an appearance. An institute called the Centre for Research & Policy of Extraterrestrial Relations decided ahead of time to make contact with extraterrestrials on that day through meditation by using telepathic means. This was supposedly the day when our galaxy arrived on the equator of the Milky Way Galaxy which marks the time of the midway beginning of the New Age.

Shortly after that date, I felt that it was time for me to get books out to help mankind evolved. Suddenly an inspiration came over me to write the second edition of the Pleiadian Papers and this book. During writing this book, I did research and much also came from inspiration as though information just poured into me from elsewhere. I feel it is the right time to awaken people up to the teachings that they may be able to use and help themselves grow in knowledge, that way one day we can live in harmony in a Free Enterprise on a global scale. If 50 states in the United States can united, why can't all the countries on this globe unite the same way one day?

For that to happen, the changes must come individually within each of us. We cannot rely on the leaders of nations to fix everything, we all must start now. It works from starting at the bottom, not the top.

The Quickening is upon us. This is the time when people are becoming aware that humanity and earth is entering a higher phase of activity. This acceleration is marked by the increasing intensity of global events and the rising temperature of nearly every planet in this solar system. Time seems to be speeding up, chaos rising as phenomenal shifts occur in our physical and perception realities with increasing speed. Extraterrestrial beings and the like have been making preparations for some time now to help gradually prepare mankind for the future that is to come. UFOs have been increasing and picking up momentum as people are increasingly being contacted by them. As contacts increase the messages from the extraterrestrials are spreading, gradually being disseminated throughout the masses.

Highly advanced humans some from other worlds have been working behind the scenes since the dawn of man here on this earth guiding the course of human evolution.

Mysterious strangers throughout history have showed up and quickly vanished just as quickly as they came, but first leave an impact that influences mankind in spirituality, science, arts and politics before they mysteriously vanished.

It is common for contactees to take a sudden interest in the occult sciences after having an encounter with UFOs or their occupants. In biblical times the pattern is also there. Prophets, who previously had no interest in the unknown, suddenly after an encounter with so-called angels, suddenly are on a spiritual path and want to share that knowledge with the world.

# HOW THIS ALL STARTED

I first took an interest in UFO's and extraterrestrials beings in 1985. Before that I didn't believe that they existed. When I was 7 years of age while our family was in Denver, Co. we all witness a formation of orange lights in the night sky. A flash of bright white light flashed from the orange lights. The formation then split up and flew away quickly in different directions and vanished. As a 7 year old I didn't know what was going on. I kept having repetitive dreams and thought the sky couldn't make up its mind if it wanted to be day or night. In the year 1985 I saw a documentary on television called 'Chariot of the Gods.' Seeing the history through Egyptian hieroglyphics and other cultures let me realize that they existed, but still somewhat skeptical, I didn't proceed to find out anything other than that.

During that year while I took an interest in Yoga and ESP (Extra Sensory Perception), I was in the school library doing research on ESP and spotted a book with bold letters URI on the binder of a book. I read the book and realize it was about an Israeli Psychic named Uri Geller. In the book it seemed to show the connection between the UFO and Uri's psychic abilities. This is what triggered my interest in UFOs and extraterrestrials.

During college a student introduced me to his cousin who belongs to a meditation group that honored extraterrestrials. I attended until shortly before the group disbanded.

During the years of research, I felt particularly drawn to the Pleiadians. Back in 1985 I read a real eye opener, 'The Andreasson Affair.' In 1992 I finally had phone contact with Betty Andreasson Luca who the UFO experience in The Andreasson Affair.' was about.

I was determined to get the teachings of the message of what the extraterrestrials supposedly had to say to the world. A lot of information I received through intuition. I also had the feeling ahead of time that I will meet Mrs. Andreasson Luca in person; I just didn't know how it would happen.

One time I was staying the night at my best friend's apartment and that is when without warning I suddenly had an experience in astral projection where when I returned to my body I felt a presence of a female, who was in her life time a Russian princess. For some time I felt guidance from her and wasn't quite sure if it was my imagination or not. I thought for a second that my roommate at the time might have slipped LSD in my drink the night before the astral projection experience. Years later I realize drugs don't affect anyone a whole day later and realize the experience was real.

Years later while home I called upon angels to look out for a problem I was having with people I was letting take advantage of me. Suddenly I felt a presence of love that I didn't expect. I almost came to tears, because I didn't think at the time that anyone could have that much love for me that I experienced. I was in awe that any beings, human or beyond could have that much loving and caring for me. After that meeting the people I had an issue with never came back around. Was it coincidence or was it something else. You be the judge.

While dating a witch we both experience UFOs in the sky in the Pittsburgh area. On the night of our last date I was driving her home while my cousin was in the car following behind us. Up ahead on a dark road in a wooded area my cousin Omar and I saw a woman in white. She had blonde hair and was solid as any normal person. I notice it was kind of odd for a woman to just stand almost in the middle of the road. I looked in the review mirror and saw the woman disappear in thin air with my own eyes. My cousin said he looked right into her green eyes and an overwhelming emotion of sadness washed over him as he witness her disappear as he looked at her.

My cousin Jim and I went to a Farm in Ford city to visit his girlfriend. She told us about her experiences and how she witness UFO's on her property. She even told us a bizarre unbelievable story of how she was pulled into another portal into her wall before she returned. After she told us this, we departed and as we drove down her long drive way, I felt an overwhelming presence of being watched. It was a little scary. Jim and I both looked at each other and he said, "Do you feel that?" I said yes, and was relieved that I wasn't the only one experiencing this. I just wanted to get out of her driveway, it frighten me some because I have never experience such a powerful presence. The driveway was so long that it seemed to take 20 minutes to reach the end of it. As we drove closer to the end, the presence started to gradually dissipate.

About a week later I took out Whitley Strieber's book *Communion* from the public library. I found the picture of the female visitor image on the cover of his book interesting and focused on it for few minutes and felt a peace and calm and a sudden urge to go back to the farm.

For three days the urge became stronger and stronger. I could no longer resist the pull. I eventually gave in and went. This time I felt compelled to pick my cousin Omar up (who we both experience the woman in white) to go with me. Omar, my cousin's girlfriend, who herself had a UFO experience when she was seven and I went to the farm in Ford City. Later when we was about to leave the farm, a UFO appeared. It appeared in a large open space in the sky and then suddenly it vanished. It came and went immediately. It had a lot of lights around it and what I saw in that short time kind of reminded me of a wedding cake.

From that experience I decided to contact a friend from the meditation group I haven't heard from since 1985. I sent her a copy of a manuscript I had written. My friend read it and as she returned it, she wrote back and left a telephone number of a yoga instructor. I contacted the yoga instructor that she suggested. The yoga instructor introduced me to information that was supposedly written by a contactee who claimed to have contact with humans from the Pleiades. The information is supposedly firsthand information directly coming from the Pleiadians about spirituality, esoteric knowledge and what's really going on about the governments and other world events. Through this I have been well educated and had contact with some people with the same source. During a speech in Denver, Colorado, I actually met Betty Andreasson Luca, her husband and her daughter Becky. Becky grew up having constant communication with extraterritorial beings. Something that she learned from the beings she shared with me that helped benefits some things in my life. I also met other contactees that given me insight and a major contact who claims to have contact with beings from the heart of Orion.

Years later when I became a practitioner of Witchcraft I felt the presence of Lilith. The air was thick with electricity and I could barely walk as I stumbled across the floor to my bed.

Later while staying at my best friend's apartment, I was switching through the channels and saw a name of a movie that had the title that was identical to my witch name. The movie was ending and it was about Lilith. The next day I ran across a lady in a witch store and we exchanged numbers. This lady had the same witch name as me and her birth surname was the same as the actress that played Lilith in the movie I saw the ending of the night before.

As I talked to this lady on the phone, she eventually told me about her experience with Lilith without her even knowing anything about my experience. When Lilith appeared to her she had blonde hair dressed in white riding on a white horse. I was surprised about her encounter. As we continued to talk she mentioned about a book that she would like to get. This book can only be purchased by members of a magical order, but neither of us could remember the name. When she mentioned the book, I recall seeing it online but didn't remember who supported it.

In the following days I was in Philadelphia on my way into walking into a witch store, there was a commotion with police inside. As I walked into the store, instead of being distracted by the commotion as most people would have, I suddenly turned my head to the left as if someone called me, but there was no audible sound. As I turned my head to see what pulled me that way I was drawn to a book I saw from a distance called Lilith's Dream by

Whitley Strieber. I walked over to open the book and Lilith was portrayed as an alien from the Pleiades. The cloak and her description kind of remind me of the witch girl who had contact with Lilith in white. I was even more determined to get the book we couldn't remember what source supported it. After that when I watched my sister's house while she was on vacation, I had a dream that lead me to a website that had the book the girl and I discussed that we didn't remember who supported it. When I woke up and saw the group that supported that book, I then became a member of the secret magical group. Right after I joined, Lilith came to me in a dream and let me know, that I don't have to settle for less in my life like I have been doing. From all of this, I felt my calling was to share and disseminate the esoteric teachings through my writing and giving lectures as my way to be part of the team that is preparing the world for the Golden Age.

# Bibliography

*The Pleiadian Papers* by Ed Russo a book on taking personal responsibility based on the teachings of the Pleiadians.

*Sacred Sexuality* by Muata Ashby D.D., P.C. On tantric spirituality as told by the ancient Egyptian tradition.

*How to make anyone fall in love with you* by Leil Lowndes is an excellent book on telling you the principles needed to make anyone fall in love with you.

*Sorcery* by J. Finely Hurley a scientific explanation of quantum entanglement that explains how telepathy and hypnosis works, and how both combined can be used.

*The 7 habits of Highly Effective People* by Stephen R. Covey explains the steps necessary to solve your interpersonal and professional problems.

*Satan an autobiography* by Yehuda Berg explains how your ego gets in the way and how to prevent it from getting in your way of receiving Light.

*Rebooting defeating depression with the power of kabbalah* by Yehuda Berg shows how you can restart your brain with desire and Light to overcome depression.

Pleiadian Spirals of Light

*The Holographic Universe* by Michael Talbot this is an excellent book that explains the inner workings of Divine Source and explains the paranormal abilities of the mind.

*Wheels of Life* by Anodea Judith, PH.D. another book that explains how to develop the Chakras

*How to Refuse to Make Yourself Miserable about Anything: Yes Anything!* By Albert Ellis PH.D. a rational approach on how to remain sane in an insane world.

*Tarot Shadow Work: Using the Dark Symbols to Heal* by Christine Jettey shows how to acknowledge the shadow self in order to become whole. One must recognize the darkness before they see the light.

*The Assertiveness Workbook: How to Express Your Ideas and Stand Up for Yourself at Work and in Relationships* by Randy J. Paterson PH.D. A workbook that shows you how to stand up for yourself and get your needs met.

www.naohide.org A website that discusses the seven Noahide laws of Noah.

*Exploring the world of Lucid Dreaming* by Stephen LaBerge, Ph.D & Howard Rheingold. A simple to do workbook that tells you what to do to have lucid dreams.

CPSIA information can be obtained
at www.ICGtesting.com
Printed in the USA
FSHW010617090921
84653FS